T0334905

Indicator Plant Species in Canadian Forests

Gordon S. Ringius and Richard A. Sims
Plant Illustrations by Susan J. Meades

Published by
Canadian Forest Service
Natural Resources Canada
Ottawa

© Her Majesty the Queen in Right of Canada, 1998
ISBN 0-660-17469-3
Cat. no. Fo42-264/1998E

Published by the Canadian Forest Service, Natural Resources Canada,
580 Booth Street, Ottawa, Ontario K1A 0E4.

All rights reserved. No part of this book may be reproduced, stored in a
retrieval system or transmitted in any form or by any means, electronic,
mechanical, photocopying, recording or otherwise without prior written
permission of the publisher.

Cette publication est aussi disponible en français sous le titre
Plantes indicatrices des forêts canadiennes.

Authors: Gordon S. Ringius and Richard A. Sims
Illustrator: Susan J. Meades
Botanical Editors: Ken Baldwin, Ken Farr, and Sheila Walsh
Managing Editor/Text Editor: Catherine Carmody
Editorial Assistant: Francine Langevin
Graphic Designer: Danielle Monette
Photo credits: Cover and pages 95, 139, and 163, photos by Maureen Carmody;
  back cover inset and on page 15, photos by Anthony Scullion.

Canadian Cataloguing in Publication Data

Ringius, Gordon S., 1949–

Indicator plant species in Canadian forests

Issued also in French under title: Plantes indicatrices
des forêts canadiennes.
Includes bibliographical references.
ISBN 0-660-17469-3; 0-660-16823-5 (softcover)
Cat. no. Fo42-264/1997-1998E

1. Plant indicators—Canada.
2. Forest plants—Canada.
I. Sims, R.A.
II. Meades, Sue, 1949–
III. Canadian Forest Service.
IV. Title.

QK938.F6R56 1996   581.7'3'0971   C97-980329-2

 Printed on
recycled paper

 PRINTED IN CANADA

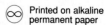 Printed on alkaline
permanent paper

Contents

Gordon S. Ringius holds an M.Sc. in biology (Acadia University, Wolfville, N.S.) and a Ph.D. in biology (University of Waterloo, Waterloo, Ont.). He was assistant curator of the herbarium at the University of Waterloo and Memorial University of Newfoundland. Currently, Dr. Ringius is owner of G.S. Ringius Associates, an environmental consulting firm, located in St. John's, Newfoundland.

Gordon S. Ringius, G.S. Ringius and Associates, Suite 66, 807 Churchill Avenue, St. John's, NF, A1A 1N7

Richard A. Sims is a senior forestry specialist with Geomatics International Inc., Vancouver, British Columbia. He has academic degrees in environmental biology (Lakehead University, Thunder Bay, Ont.), plant ecology (University of Manitoba, Winnipeg), and forestry (University of British Columbia, Vancouver). Previous to his present position, Dr. Sims was a research scientist for over 19 years with the Canadian Forest Service, Natural Resources Canada, where he served as a research forester, vegetational ecologist, and site/land classification specialist.

Richard A. Sims, Director, Forest Applications, Geomatics International Inc., Box 14, Suite 720, 1140 West Pender Street, Vancouver, BC, V6E 4G1

Susan J. Meades is a free-lance botanist and botanical illustrator. She has an M.Sc. in botany and has illustrated or contributed to several publications in forestry and environmental science. Before moving to Sault Ste. Marie, Ontario, in 1995, Ms. Meades lived in Flatrock, Newfoundland. She is currently working on a field guide to the native flora of Newfoundland.

Susan J. Meades, Box 14, Peace Tree Drive, Sault Ste. Marie, ON, P6A 5K7

We would like to thank the following people for providing information and suggestions during the preparation of this report: **Phil Comeau** and **Andrew MacKinnon**, technical advisor and research scientist, respectively, with the British Columbia Forest Service; **Vincent F. Zelazny**, forester with the New Brunswick Department of Natural Resources and Energy; **Robert R. Ireland**, bryologist with the Canadian Museum of Nature, Ottawa; and **Doyle Wells**, research scientist with the Canadian Forest Service (CFS) in St. John's, Newfoundland.

Background information on many species was researched by **Sheila Walsh**, CFS, Sault Ste. Marie. **Ken Baldwin**, CFS, Sault Ste. Marie, coordinated the final review of the manuscript and assessed and incorporated the suggested changes; his diligence and dedication made the realization of this publication possible. **Ken Farr**, CFS, Ottawa, also contributed to the final drafting of the manuscript in addition to developing a glossary of selected technical terms and researching and overseeing the production of the range maps. Technical assistance was given by **Bobbie-Jo Rowlinson**, CFS, Sault Ste. Marie. Review comments were provided by **Guy Brassard**, CFS, Ottawa; **Ken Baldwin**, CFS, Sault Ste. Marie; **Ian Corns**, CFS, Edmonton: and **Ole Hendrickson**, CFS, Ottawa. We also gratefully acknowledge the contribution of **Marc Favreau**, Translation Services, Public Works and Government Services, whose patience, attention to detail, and botanical knowledge while translating the English manuscript have contributed to quality of the publication in both languages.

Susan J. Meades produced the original line drawings used to illustrate the 80 species included in this publication; her drawings and her review of the species factsheets have contributed substantially to the book.

Funding for the preparation of this publication was provided by the Ecological Land Classification (ELC) initiative of the federal Green Plan, and the work was overseen and administered by the Canadian Forest Service's ELC Steering Committee.

Chairperson

Dr. Richard Sims
Natural Resources Canada
Canadian Forest Service
Great Lake Forestry Centre
Sault Ste. Marie, ON P6A 5M7

Secretary

Dr. Ole Hendrickson
Natural Resources Canada
Canadian Forest Service
Ottawa, ON K1A 0E4

Members

Dr. Louis Archambault
Natural Resources Canada
Canadian Forest Service
Laurentian Forestry Centre
Ste-Foy, PQ G1V 4C7

Ken Baldwin
Natural Resources Canada
Canadian Forest Service
Great Lakes Forestry Centre
Sault Ste. Marie, ON P6A 5M7

Dr. Ian Corns
Natural Resources Canada
Canadian Forest Service
Northern Forestry Centre
Edmonton, AB T6H 3S5

Dr. Luc Duchesne
Petawawa National Forestry Institute
Chalk River, ON K0J 1J0

Dr. Karel Klinka
Faculty of Forestry
University of British Columbia
Vancouver, BC V6T 1W5

Dr. Taumey Mahendrappa
Natural Resources Canada
Canadian Forest Service
Atlantic Forestry Centre
Fredericton, NB E3B 5P7

Dr. Bruce Roberts
Natural Resources Canada
Canadian Forest Service
Atlantic Forestry Centre
St. John's, NF A1C 5X8

Peter Uhlig
Ontario Forest Research Institute
Ontario Ministry of Natural Resources
Sault Ste. Marie, ON P6A 5N5

Note: This list reflects membership on the committee in 1995, at the time the manuscript was finalized.

Forest resource managers in Canada are just beginning to recognize the value of many forest floor and understory plant species for assessing forest site quality. The potential and/or limitations of a site for producing future crops of commercial trees are difficult to forecast when crop trees are absent due to clearcutting, fire, windthrow, or other disturbances. Direct measures of site quality are time-consuming and expensive. Plant species that convey information about the ecological nature of a site, however, offer alternative methods of site evaluation. These plants are known as indicator species.

Indicator plant species are proving valuable as site evaluation tools in forest resource management. A wide variety of site conditions including soil nutrient and moisture regimes, forest humus types, soil reaction (pH level), and general soil type (organic or mineral) can be determined from the presence of a plant species. For example, plants known as nitrophytes indicate nitrogen-rich soils, calciphytes calcium-rich soils. Some species are sensitive to the general dryness or wetness of a site; they indicate whether the site (or microhabitats within the site) tends to shed water, receive water, or collect water, and whether it is characterized by a fluctuating water table.

This publication is an introduction to the concept of plants as indicators of environmental conditions within Canada's forests. It provides information on the identification, ecology, geographic range, and indicator value of 80 selected forest plant species— vascular plants, mosses, and lichens. The species were selected as examples of plant indicators for a range of forest site conditions across Canada; they do not constitute an exhaustive list of forest indicator species. As knowledge increases and as forest managers come to recognize the ecological relevance of non-timber plant species, a more comprehensive series of descriptions of a much larger set of indicator species will have to be developed. We expect that these species will become important tools for resource management planning. Further investigations may also lead to the derivation of an important set of species-based indices that could be used to identify and monitor critical characteristics of forest biodiversity.

We hope this guide will increase awareness of forest vegetation and its importance to forest management practices in Canada. It should also be of interest to resource planners, foresters, ecologists, botanists, naturalists and anyone who wishes to know more about forest plants and the sites they occupy.

Methodology

We began preparation of this guide by developing a list of potential indicator forest plant species. Practising foresters, ecologists, and botanists from across Canada submitted names of species that they felt qualified as good indicators of certain environmental variables. The result was a list of approximately 120 candidate species. For each of these species, information on the following traits was gathered and summarized in tabular form:

• Indicator value
• Strength of indicator value
• Other species with similar indicator value
• Distribution
• Commonness
• Miscellaneous attributes

A final group of 80 species was selected from the preliminary list. These species were considered to best represent a full range of indicator values, forest cover types, and species distributions across the country.

The language of this guide is as non-technical as possible. However, the use of some technical terms, particularly in the taxonomic descriptions, is unavoidable for the sake of accuracy and conciseness. Definitions for some of these terms can be found in the **Glossary**. Publications from which technical information was derived are listed in the **References**.

Plants as Indicators of Environmental Conditions

Numerous studies have shown that indicator species can be effective predictors of forest ecological conditions. Pregitzer and Barnes (1982) found that certain forest plant species in Michigan were strongly associated with shallow soils. These same authors were also able to show that indicator species could be used, with a known probability of error, to classify soil drainage. Common moss species have proven to be good indicators of soil pH levels on mesic and hydric sites (Robinson et al. 1982). In an early study of indicator species, Hazard (1937) reported that forest floor vegetation in general indicates soil fertility; more recently, Pregitzer and Barnes (1982) found ground flora to be sensitive to small changes in soil fertility. Indicator plant species, through their presence, relative abundance, and vigor on a site, provide important clues about a site's environmental characteristics.

Plant communities comprise numerous species combinations. Each plant species is adapted to a range of environmental conditions under which it can persist and reproduce; thus, each species occurs only within its own limits of ecological tolerance (Daubenmire 1976; Klinka et al. 1989). By knowing the ecological requirements of plant species, information about the physical and chemical environment found in association with particular species can be inferred.

Since all plant species occur within specific ecological limits, every species could theoretically be considered as an "indicator" of environmental, site, physical, and/or chemical conditions within its tolerance range. The strength of a plant species' indicator value is determined by the degree of correlation between its occurrence on a site and the values of the environmental variable(s) for which the plant is considered an indicator. Most plant species are normally distributed along a set of environmental gradients. This can be represented graphically for a single hypothetical variable (Figure 1).

For a given environmental variable, a normally distributed species will show peak performance at some value (optimum) along the gradient and decreasing performance in either direction away from the optimum. Eventually, values will be reached that are too low (minimum) or too high (maximum) for the species to persist and reproduce. The range of values from the minimum to the maximum for a given environmental variable is the ecological amplitude for that species on that variable. The narrower a species' ecological amplitude is for a given variable, the better an indicator the species is for that variable. When the ecological amplitude of a particular species is well understood for some environmental variable (from previous research), its performance on a site can be predicted by determining the quality of the site with respect to that variable. For example if a species with a strong preference for acidic soils, such as mayflower (*Epigaea repens*), is introduced to a site that was determined to be strongly

Figure 1.

Theoretical representation of a species' ecological amplitude along a hypothetical environmental gradient. Response curves for species with wide and narrow ecological amplitudes are also illustrated.

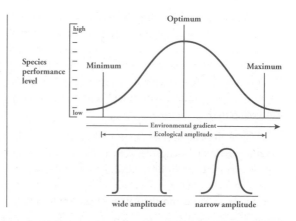

basic in soil reaction, one would predict that this species would perform poorly.

Conversely, if a species with a known, narrow, ecological amplitude for a given environmental variable is found to occur on a site, then it should be possible to predict the quality of the site with respect to that variable. For example, the presence of bulblet fern (*Cystopteris bulbifera*), a known calciphyte, on a site would allow one to predict with reasonable certainty that the soil on the site is rich in calcium. In other words, each plant species is adapted to a certain range of environmental conditions and, by the same token, is restricted to sites that fall within that range.

To make an accurate determination of site qualities, the indicator plant species should be relatively common and healthy on the sample site. Sporadic occurrences of some species, often associated with low cover and low vigor (and usually limited to special microsites), can be encountered at or slightly beyond their ecological minima and maxima. In such cases, the site assessment must be augmented by consideration of other species on the site. For example, where there has been a recent change in the environment, a species, once thriving on a site, might now be represented only by non-reproducing, relict individuals and be facing extirpation from the site. For this reason (and others) rare plants generally do not make good indicator species (Rowe 1956).

The use of plant species as indicators of site quality is currently limited by a lack of detailed information on the ecology and distribution of native plants. Environmental relationships (and thus, predictive value) of individual species may vary geographically in response to climatic, physiographic, and genetic variations, with the result that ecotypes may be formed within a single species (Strong et al. 1991). The extent and nature of ecotype formation must be understood for each indicator species. Until this information is available, species information obtained in one area cannot be extrapolated to uninvestigated areas. Competitive interactions among the different co-occurring species must also be studied. Plant associations with different mixtures of species could result in shifting of the species' ecological optima along certain environmental gradients (Klinka et al. 1989). For example, in the presence of a competitor, an indicator species may be confined to a restricted portion of an environmental gradient, but when the competing species is removed or replaced by another, the indicator species may broaden out along the gradient or shift its ecological optimum to another position. The use of indicator plant species for determining site qualities requires care and intelligent observation.

Significance of Indicator Plants to Forest Management

Indicator species have provided reliable information to practitioners in a variety of disciplines across Canada. In agriculture, soil scientists and agronomists have used indicator species to assess soil properties (Swanson and Grigal 1989), various edaphic factors (Pregitzer and Barnes 1982), and range conditions (Wroe et al. 1979). Engineers have used indicator species to help avoid drainage problems during road and site construction (Comeau et al. 1982), and geologists have identified many species that are useful in mineral exploration (Carlisle et al. 1986; Strong et al. 1991). Biologists have used indicator species for years to monitor environmental pollution levels (Addison and Puckett 1980; Puckett and Finegan 1980; Nieboer et al. 1978; Hawksworth and Rose 1970).

Forest resource managers have always been keenly interested in developing means to assess the quality of forest sites. Information on a site's productive potential has important practical and economic implications; forest managers want to be able to identify sites that will give the best return on management efforts. Resource managers must also be able to recognize the limitations of a site in order to select practices that maintain its productive potential. Traditionally, forest site quality has been assessed either by measuring physical and chemical attributes of the soil or by collecting growth and yield data from tree species occurring on the site (Payandeh 1986). However, forest floor and understory vegetation includes many indicator species that can provide relatively precise information on most growth-related site-quality factors, even those that can be difficult to measure directly (Corns and Pluth 1984; La Roi et al 1988; Green et al. 1989; Carmean 1975).

The use of indicator plant species to determine site quality offers some distinct advantages over other means. Soil can be evaluated much more rapidly with indicator species than with costly and time-consuming pit excavations and laboratory analyses (Pregitzer and Barnes 1982; Klinka et al. 1989). Soil samples are usually few in number and limited to a single sampling period, thus making it difficult to ensure that a representative sample has been obtained. Plants, on the other hand, reflect the combined effects of climate, soil, physiography, and biota over a long and continuous period of time. They thus provide information not only on all pertinent environmental variables but also on temporal fluctuations and intervariable interactions, factors that could be important in determining site quality. On treed sites, indicator plant species offer a cost-effective alternative to growth and yield analysis. Where trees are absent, immature, or diseased, indicator species allow researchers to predict the potential productivity of a site (Strong et al. 1991).

Perhaps the most widespread use of plant indicators in forest management practice in Canada is within the context of ecological forest site classification. Site classification is a necessary precondition for effective forest resource management. It provides the foundation for collecting and interpreting research results and can provide a basis for extrapolating management techniques to new sites. In the early 1900s, forest ecologists demonstrated that plants, either individually or in groups of species, could indicate general habitat conditions by reflecting the influences of many environmental and site factors (Pregitzer and Barnes 1982). Much of this work was pioneered by A.K. Cajander (1926), a forester working on forest sites in Finland. By the late 1920s, researchers in Canada had demonstrated that boreal forest understory vegetation was closely correlated with soil moisture and soil nutrient regimes (Rowe 1992). Similar findings were being reported for forests in the northeastern United States. For example, Heimberger (1934) reported relationships between plant species composition and soil conditions in Adirondack forests, and Hazard (1937) found that ground vegetation in white pine stands could be used to classify these forests on the basis of potential natural productivity. The relationships between forest understory vegetation, soil conditions, and site quality provided the basis for the earliest forest site classification efforts in Canada (Rowe 1992).

More recently, forest vegetation has been combined with soil, climate, and physiographic factors in ecologically based site classification systems (e.g., Corns and Annas 1986; Jones et al. 1983; Meades and Moores 1989; Sims et al. 1989). These regional forest ecosystem classifications are unique in their specific terminologies and methodologies and are applicable only in the geographic areas for which they were developed. All, however, share similar concepts and ideologies and provide an invaluable ecological framework for the description, assessment, and consequently better management of Canada's forests.

Guide to Species Factsheets

Each species factsheet uses a two-page format. The factsheet layout is shown in Figure 2 and the information categories are explained below:

1. Species Name

The scientific name of each species, with its botanical author, is provided at the top of the left-hand page. Nomenclature in this report follows these works: for vascular plants, *The Flora of Canada* (Scoggan 1978); for mosses, *Mosses of Eastern North America* (Crum and Anderson 1981), and *Some*

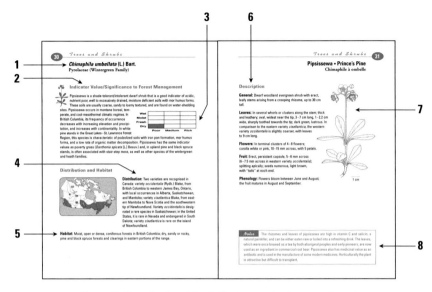

Figure 2. Organization of the indicator species two-page layout.

Common Mosses of British Columbia (Schofield 1969); and for lichens, *How to Know the Lichens* (Hale 1979). Other scientific names (synonyms) which have been applied to the same species in recent botanical references are included at the bottom of the **Description** category (6). Common names in both English and French are provided at the top of the right-hand page of the factsheet. Only names in common and widespread usage are included. The common English, French and scientific names of most species referred to in the publication are listed in the **appendix**.

2. Indicator Value/Significance to Forest Management

Indicator value is a statement on a perceived correlation between the presence of a species on a site and some environmental variable associated with the site (Klinka et al. 1989). The strength of a species' indicator value is determined by its ecological amplitude for the indicated environmental variable (see Figure 1). The term "characteristic" implies a weaker correlation between a species and its indicated environmental variable than the term "indicator". The term "indicator" may be modified by qualitative adjectives such as "moderate", "good", or "excellent", depending on the strength of the correlation.

This category also includes information on shade tolerance and specific soil nutrient, moisture, or reaction preferences of the species. Shade tolerance is described using three relative, qualitative classes: shade-intolerant (the species requires direct sunlight), shade-tolerant/intolerant (the species is capable of growing under both shaded and full light regimes), and shade-tolerant (the species requires shade). General climatic regimes (including elevation and latitude relationships) (Klinka et al. 1989), as well as forest types and regions (Rowe 1972), within which the species occurs are indicated. Common species associates and species with similar indicator values are listed. Plant species not described in the publication are always accompanied by their scientific name. Scientific names are not given for tree species and genera mentioned in the context of stand or forest type.

Statements on forest humus form are restricted to the order level of generalization, in which three internationally accepted terms—mor, moder, and mull—are used (Luttmerding et al. 1990; Sims and Baldwin 1996). These terms are defined in the **Glossary**. Topographic position in relation to soil drainage characteristics is summarized by assigning sites to one of three classes: water-shedding, water-receiving, and water-collecting (Figure 3).

Information on the species' significance to forest management considerations is included when available. Such information for non-commercial plant species is highly variable, ranging from considerable information, for species which have traditionally caused problems with regeneration and growth of commercial crop tree species, to very little information, for species believed to have no appreciable impact on forest management operations. Important considerations include competition for light, nutrients, and water at the

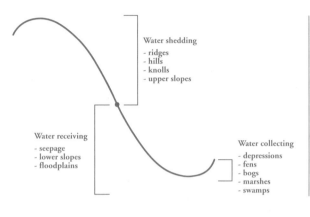

Figure 3.

Schematic cross-section of a topographic sequence illustrating the relative positions of water-shedding, water-receiving, and water-collecting sites.

various stages of crop tree development; potential for causing mechanical damage to crop tree individuals; and the capacity to act as alternate hosts for crop tree pests. Additional information will accumulate for the more poorly documented species as non-commercial plants become used more frequently as indicators by foresters, ecologists, and others working in Canada's forests.

3. Edatopic Grid

For each species, an edatopic grid provides a two-dimensional cross-tabulation between soil moisture regime and soil nutrient regime on a characteristic site occupied by the species. The soil moisture regime represents the long-term balance between the amount of water available and the demand for that water by plants on a site (Klinka et al. 1989). It is divided into four subjectively defined classes: dry, fresh, moist, and wet—classes that have been traditionally used in Canada for forest site classification (e.g., see Mueller-Dombois 1964; Rowe 1956). The soil nutrient regime indicates the average levels of essential soil nutrients that are available to plants on a site over several years (Klinka et al. 1989). It is represented by three subjectively defined classes:

poor, medium, and rich. On the edatopic grids provided in the species factsheets, the vertical axes refer to soil moisture regime and the horizontal axes to soil nutrient regime. Within a given climate, soil moisture regime and soil nutrient regime are important determinants of site quality (Coile 1938; Kimmins 1987). The edatopic grid provides a graphic summary of soil moisture and nutrient regimes and permits a quick, simplified assessment of site quality conditions under which a species is found.

4. Distribution

The geographic distribution of each species is described and mapped. The text description allows for treatment of recognized subspecies and varieties; when possible the geographic distributions of these infraspecific variants are provided. Reference to forest regions is derived from Rowe (1972). The legally designated rare and endangered status for species that are protected in various jurisdictions is given. The distribution maps provide a rapid means of determining the geographic range of a species in Canada. Most of the maps were adapted from previously published maps found in botanical references, although a few were developed from text descriptions given in Scoggan (1978).

5. Habitat

A brief description is given for the most likely habitats of each species. The descriptions were taken from references covering the complete geographic range of the species. Known shifts in habitat preference from one part of a species' range to another are noted.

6. Description

Species descriptions are intended as aids to the identification of the indicator species. The species have been organized into four groups, representing recognizable growth forms: trees and shrubs; herbs and grasses; ferns and fern-allies; and mosses and lichens. For every species, there is a general description stating what the whole plant looks like and noting any significant features of its overall growth habit. With the exception of the *Cladina* spp.

and woodland horsetail (*Equisetum sylvaticum*) factsheets, every species also contains a more detailed description of leaf characteristics. For trees, shrubs, and herbs, the species description is completed with information on flowers and fruit. For grasses, a single paragraph describing the inflorescence is presented. Factsheets for ferns, fern-allies, and mosses contain descriptions of the various reproductive structures found in these plant forms. Only one lichen genus, *Cladina*, is included in this report and it is represented by several species. They are treated together on one factsheet with general descriptions only.

Some of the terminology and anatomical structures for nonflowering plants may be unfamiliar to readers. Well-illustrated information on fern and fern-ally morphology is available in B. Cobb's (1963) *A Field Guide to the Ferns*. Illustrations of moss morphology can be found in W.B. Schofield's (1969) *Some Common Mosses of British Columbia*. M.E. Hale's (1979) second edition of *How to Know the Lichens* offers an excellent introduction to lichen morphology and methods of identification. For additional taxonomic information on any species contained in this report, refer to the titles with asterisks in the **References**.

The **Description** category of the factsheet finishes with phenological information about flowering and fruiting periods. Some flowering species bloom for only a few days each year (usually those appearing in the early spring before leaf emergence in the forest canopy), while others have a protracted period of blooming, which may last all summer. Flowering time is given as a range between two dates. Generally, flowering begins in the southern portion of a species' range and progresses northward over a period of a few days or weeks. When available, regional information is provided for the flowering times. Fruit maturation refers to the time when fruits are ripe and the seeds ready for dispersal. This generally occurs a few weeks after flowering. Again, a range of dates is provided. Note that flowering and fruiting are greatly influenced by weather conditions. Early or late springs can hasten or postpone the phenology of a species by several weeks in any given year.

7. Line Drawings

Each species is illustrated by a line drawing or set of drawings. The drawings were prepared from examination of fresh material, herbarium specimens, and photographs. All drawings were rendered by one artist so that quality and style are consistent throughout the report. Each illustration contains a drawing of the entire plant or a representative portion of the plant. For many species, flowers, fruits, or other diagnostic plant structures are also illustrated. The size of the plant or detailed part is indicated by a scale bar. Where there is only one scale bar, it refers to all drawings within the illustration.

8. Notes

Most factsheets conclude with general comments on known cultural or wildlife uses, edibility, and toxicity. **Please be aware that we do not recommend any of the noted uses nor the consumption of wild plants based on the information in this guide.**

Trees
and
Shrubs

Acer circinatum Pursh
Aceraceae (Maple Family)

Indicator Value/Significance to Forest Management

Vine maple is a shade-tolerant/intolerant shrub that is a moderate indicator of nutrient rich, fresh to moist sites, in cool-mesothermal climates, particularly where the soil nitrogen content is high and moder and mull humus forms are present. The leaf litter of this species is nutrient rich and promotes the development of moder humus forms, which are favorable to the productive growth of many conifer crop species. An associated species with similar indiator value is sword fern. Vine maple becomes less frequent with increasing elevation and continentality. This species is dominant in primary successional stages on water-shedding sites with colluvial soils, and is abundant in open-canopy forests and clearings on water-receiving sites.

	Poor	Medium	Rich
Wet			
Moist			▓
Fresh			▓
Dry			

Vine maple has the potential to be a very strong competitor, especially on nutrient rich sites where it regenerates quickly after logging or slash fires. Because of its rapid initial growth, this species could seriously interfere with Douglas-fir (*Pseudotsuga menziesii* [Mirb.] Franco) establishment. It does not, however, occur widely in British Columbia and thus creates competition problems only in localized areas.

Distribution and Habitat

Distribution: In the Coast Forest Region; confined to submontane and montane habitats on the mainland of southwestern British Columbia and 2 small areas on Vancouver Island.

Habitat: Most often on fresh to very moist, rocky, alluvial soils along streams; also found in coniferous forests and forest openings, particularly in recently harvested areas.

Vine Maple
Érable circiné

Description

General: Short, crooked, deciduous shrub or tree, up to 9 m tall, with few twisted, spreading branches supporting a low, broad, irregular crown; trunk often prostrate or arching, rooting where it contacts the ground.

Leaves: Opposite; maple-leaf shape with nearly circular outline, 6–11 cm across, usually with 7–9 lobes, occasionally 5; with conspicuous veins radiating from the leaf base; lobes narrowly triangular, toothed, separated by V-shaped notches; bright yellowish-green above, pale green below.

Flowers: In loose drooping clusters **(a)** from the tips of small branches; petals present; flowers with both male and female parts but only one sex is functional in each flower.

Fruit: A samara, 2.5–4 cm long, wings wide-spreading to form nearly a straight line **(b)**; seed-containing portion of the samara swollen and prominently ridged.

Phenology: Flowers bloom from March to June, appearing with the leaves or when the leaves are half grown; the fruit ripens from September to October, at which time the stalks turn and the samaras stand erect above the leaves; seed dispersal takes place from September to January.

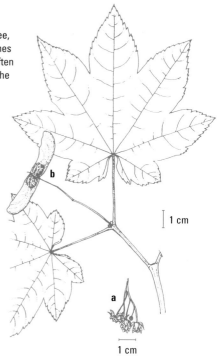

1 cm

1 cm

Notes Like most maple species, vine maple has considerable ornamental value, particularly in its native area. It has features of interest for every season—attractive flowers in spring, tinted leaves in summer that turn brilliant orange and scarlet in fall, and contorted, twisted branches that make interesting silhouettes in winter.

Alnus crispa (Ait.) Pursh
Betulaceae (Birch Family)

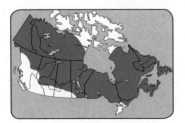

Indicator Value/Significance to Forest Management

Green alder is a nitrogen-fixing, shade-intolerant shrub characteristic of dry to fresh, moderately to coarsely textured mineral soils. It is tolerant of a range of moisture conditions on well to poorly drained soils; although tolerant of spring flooding, it is intolerant of stagnant water and drought. Generally, green alder is better adapted to drier site conditions than other species of alder. Its nutrient requirements appear to be low, although it grows well on moderately rich sites, and it occurs more frequently on coarse-textured sands and loams

than on fine-textured silts and clays. In spruce stands in the northwestern Boreal Forest Region, it is characteristic of upslope sites with shallow soils and relatively open canopies.

Green alder may compete with coniferous crop regeneration by shading seedlings and competing for soil moisture. Competition is greatest on sites with moderately well-drained to imperfectly drained soils. On such sites green alder is often well-established in the understory and can become a major competitor after harvesting; shrub control may be required on these sites. In winter, green alder may also cause mechanical damage to crop tree seedlings if its stems are bent down by snow. Green alder is capable of improving soil conditions by adding organic matter, and of increasing the soil nitrogen content through its ability to fix atmospheric nitrogen. These features give it good potential for acting as a nurse crop for timber production on sterile sites. In some instances, it may benefit conifer seedling growth by suppressing competition from bluejoint grass and *Rubus* spp.(brambles). By rapidly colonizing disturbed sites, it stabilizes soil, thereby reducing soil erosion.

Distribution and Habitat

Distribution: Yukon, Northwest Territories, northern British Columbia, east to Newfoundland.

Habitat: In dry–fresh upland forest habitats, on disturbed ground, on sandy or gravelly slopes and flats, and along roadsides; also forms thickets along streams, lakeshores, coasts, and wetland margins.

Green Alder
Aulne crispé

Description

General: Deciduous shrub 1–3 m tall, stems ascending and curving outwards from the base, older branches with smooth, grayish bark; buds sessile.

Leaves: Alternate; round-oval to ovate in shape, 2–8 cm long, rounded or slightly heart-shaped at the base; margins finely sharp-toothed; cross veins not continuous **(a)**.

Flowers: Catkins; both sexes on the same plant; at anthesis, male catkins drooping from the ends of the branches, 4–6 cm long, yellowish; at pollination, female catkins erect, 1–1.5 cm long, green with reddish styles. Only the male catkins **(b)** are exposed in winter, approximately 1 cm long; female catkins are protected within the buds.

Fruit: Small, winged nutlets borne in stalked, oval-shaped, woody "cones" (mature female catkins).

Phenology: Flowering occurs during April and May as the leaves expand; nutlets mature in the fall; woody "cones" **(c)** often persist on the shrub for a year or more. Only the male catkins appear during the previous growing season.

Synonym: *Alnus viridis* (Chaix) DC. ssp. *crispa* (Ait.) Turrill

---

Notes   Green alder provides browse for moose, caribou, and snowshoe hare, although it is not a preferred food source. The leaf and flower buds of green alder are rich in bitter compounds that may render the foliage unpalatable.

Alnus rugosa (Du Roi) Spreng.
Betulaceae (Birch Family)

Indicator Value/Significance to Forest Management

Speckled alder is a nitrogen-fixing, shade-intolerant shrub that is a good indicator of poorly drained soils. It typically forms thickets on sites where surface drainage is slow and where the water table is near the surface during the early growing season. On better drained lands this species is associated with seep-age. Later in the season these sites may become relatively dry. Speckled alder grows well on a wide variety of soils, including rocky till, sandy loam, gray forest soils, muck, and well-drained clay soils. It is commonly associated with black spruce stands in

	Poor	Medium	Rich
Wet		▓	
Moist		▓	
Fresh			
Dry			

the eastern part of the Boreal Forest Region, although not in the Atlantic portion; in wet habitats in the Northern Clay Section of northern Ontario, this species is a sensitive indicator of miner-otrophy.

Speckled alder enhances the nitrogen content of soils and this enrichment may be beneficial to conifer crop development. A sparse shrub layer by alder may check the growth of dense sward-forming grasses, such as bluejoint grass, thereby increasing seedling survival rates. On susceptible sites it may be used as a nurse crop to lessen the risk of frost heaving. Speckled alder may be detrimental to conifer crop production, particularly on fresh and moist sites, if its canopy cover is dense and crop seedlings are shaded. Harvesting of balsam fir (*Abies balsamea* [L.] Mill.) and spruce (*Picea* spp.) on wet sites is sometimes followed by the development of dense thickets of speckled alder.

Distribution and Habitat

Distribution: Yukon, east to Labrador and central Newfoundland.

Habitat: Grows best in relatively wet low-lying habitats such as margins of wetlands, streambanks, lakeshores, often forming dense thickets; very common in wet black spruce forests on organic soils.

Speckled Alder
Aulne rugueux

Description

General: Coarse deciduous shrub or small tree, usually less than 4 m tall; stems clumped from the base or solitary, crooked, always with a wide curve at the base; older branches with smooth reddish-brown bark and whitish to grayish lenticels; buds stalked.

Leaves: Alternate; oval, 5–10 cm long; thick textured, wrinkled above, with 10 or more pairs of veins, cross-veins prominent forming a ladder-like pattern **(a)**; margins double-toothed, undulating.

Flowers: Catkins; both sexes on the same plant; at anthesis, male catkins drooping from the ends of the branches, 4–6 cm long, yellowish; at pollination, female catkins erect, 1–1.5 cm long, green with reddish styles. Both male **(b)** and female **(c)** catkins are visible in the winter, much smaller than when expanded in spring.

Fruit: Small, winged nutlets borne in nearly sessile, oval-shaped, woody "cones" **(d)** (mature female catkins).

Phenology: Flowering occurs during April and May before the leaves expand; nutlets mature in the fall. Woody "cones" often persist on the shrub for a year or more. Both male and female catkins appear during the previous growing season.

Synonym: *Alnus incana* ssp. *rugosa* (Du Roi) J. Clausen

> **Notes** Many species of wildlife, including moose, deer, muskrat, beaver, cottontail, and snowshoe hare, feed on the twigs and foliage of speckled alder. Seeds and buds are consumed by grouse and song birds. Speckled alder thickets provide important shelter for grouse and woodcock. The branches are sometimes used by beaver in the construction of dams. Dyes can be obtained from various parts of the plant—the roots produce a brown dye and the bark gives a yellowish to reddish dye.

Andromeda glaucophylla Link
Ericaceae (Heath Family)

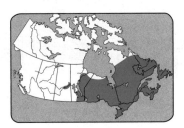

Indicator Value/Significance to Forest Management

Bog-rosemary is a good indicator of acidic, nutrient poor, wet organic soils. These soils are found in water-collecting sites with large accumulations of peat, and occur under boreal, cool-temperate, and cool-mesothermal climatic regimes.

	Poor	Medium	Rich
Wet	■		
Moist			
Fresh			
Dry			

Other species with similar indicator values include leatherleaf, bog-laurel, and sphagnum mosses. Bog-rosemary is found in open bogs and fens, often in association with black spruce and tamarack. In the Hudson Bay Lowlands and southern parts of the Boreal Forest Region in northern Ontario, this species is a rich fen indicator, sensitive to the presence of minerotrophic soil conditions.

Distribution and Habitat

Distribution: Saskatchewan, east to Labrador and Newfoundland. Bog-rosemary is a designated rare species in Saskatchewan; in the United States, it has been extirpated in Illinois, and it is designated endangered in West Virginia, threatened in Rhode Island, and rare in New Jersey and Connecticut.

Habitat: Wet, organic soils, especially in black spruce swamps, wetlands, and heathlands.

Bog-Rosemary
Andromède glauque

Description

General: Low, evergreen shrub, 10–70 cm tall, with ascending glaucous stems arising from a creeping rootstock; tips of the branches curved and leaves bent upward.

Leaves: Alternate; crowded towards the twig ends; linear; margins smooth, rolling towards the undersurface (**a**); leathery; whitened below with fine white hairs, dark green above (**b**).

Flowers: In nodding terminal clusters of 3–7 flowers (**c**), turning upright in fruit (**d**); corolla small, about 6 mm long, urn-shaped, white to pink with 5 rose-colored lobes.

Fruit: Flattened, globular, 5-part capsule.

Phenology: Flowers bloom in June and July.

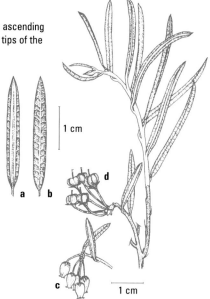

1 cm

a   b

d

c

1 cm

Notes   The leaves and twigs of bog-rosemary are used in some parts of Russia for tanning leather. The plant contains a poison, andromedotoxin, which causes low blood pressure, breathing difficulty, vomiting, diarrhea, and cramps when consumed; the toxin is especially dangerous to livestock.

Arctostaphylos uva-ursi (L.) Spreng.
Ericaceae (Heath Family)

Indicator Value/Significance to Forest Management

Bearberry is a shade-intolerant, oxylophytic, creeping shrub that is a good indicator of nutrient poor, dry to very dry soils. These moisture deficient soils tend to be acidic, developing mor humus forms on water-shedding sites under boreal, temperate, and cool-mesothermal climatic regimes. In British Columbia, its frequency of occurrence increases with increasing continentality. This species is often associated with salal, common juniper, Schreber's moss (*Pleurozium schreberi* [Brid.] Mitt.), and several species of the lichen genus *Cladina*. On Vancouver Island,

bearberry, in association with dense patches of common juniper, often indicates habitats that are too dry and soils too shallow to support tree growth. In the Boreal Forest and Great Lakes–St. Lawrence Forest Regions, bearberry is common in young, open-canopy, seral lodgepole pine and jack pine forests on well-drained, sandy to gravelly soils.

Distribution and Habitat

Distribution: Wide ranging, circumpolar species, from Yukon and Mackenzie District, N.W.T., south to southern British Columbia and east to Newfoundland. Bearberry is designated a rare species in Prince Edward Island.

Habitat: Open-canopy pine forests on dry, rapidly drained, shallow, sandy and coarse loamy soils, exposed rock outcrops, sandy plains.

Bearberry • Kinnikinnick
Raisin d'ours

Description

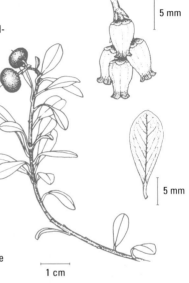

5 mm

General: Low, trailing, evergreen shrub with spreading flexible branches up to several metres long and often forming loose mats; leafy branches up to 15 cm high; mature branches smooth, dark reddish-brown or gray, with peeling papery bark.

Leaves: Alternate; 1.3–2 cm long, oval to egg-shaped, broadest towards the tip and tapering to the base; thick and leathery, shiny dark green above, paler below; margins smooth, flat to rolling slightly towards the undersurface.

5 mm

Flowers: In terminal clusters of 4–5; corolla urn-shaped, about 5 mm long, white or pinkish, with 5 rose-tinged lobes.

Fruit: Bright red, slightly flattened, berry-like drupe with dry pulp; 7–8 mm across.

1 cm

Phenology: Flowers bloom from April to June; the fruit matures by mid-August and remains on the plant throughout the winter.

Notes   Bearberries are used as a food source by bears and various species of birds. Although edible, the ripe berries are dry, mealy, and not very tasty. Some aboriginal peoples used bearberries to make a type of pemmican. When dried and powdered, the leaves have been used as a substitute for tobacco. In Sweden and Russia, the dried leaves are used medicinally as an astringent, tonic, and diuretic.

Chamaedaphne calyculata (L.) Moench
Ericaceae (Heath Family)

Indicator Value/Significance to Forest Management

Leatherleaf is a shade-intolerant, oxylophytic shrub that is a good indicator of wet, nutrient poor, organic soils. It occurs on water-collecting sites, and is common in open bogs. In the southern Boreal Forest Region in Ontario this species is indicative of very oligotrophic, low shrub and graminoid rich, treed bogs with poorly decomposed peat and a surface-level water table. In Quebec, where leatherleaf is a characteristic bog species, its high vegetative reproductive capacity allows rapid and extensive establishment of almost pure stands in which inva-sion by other species becomes difficult. It is also tolerant of fire and changes in drainage. Species with similar indicator values include bog-rosemary, bog-laurel, and Labrador-tea.

	Poor	Medium	Rich
Wet	■		
Moist			
Fresh			
Dry			

Distribution and Habitat

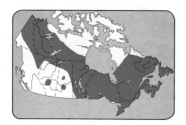

Distribution: Yukon and Northwest Territories, northern British Columbia, northern and central Alberta, northern and central Saskatchewan, Manitoba, east to Labrador and Newfoundland.

Habitat: A variety of wetlands, lake margins, and other wet habitats with abundant sunlight; often occurring in shallow water or in locations with surface-level water tables.

Leatherleaf • Cassandra
Cassandre caliculé

Description

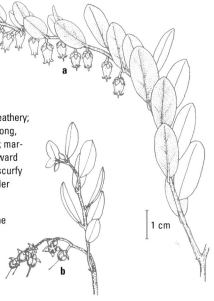

General: Much-branched, long-lived, low, evergreen shrub, usually less than 1 m tall, often forming extensive patches; twigs with arching or curved tips and covered with brown scales; older branches smooth and green to reddish-brown.

Leaves: Alternate; often overlapping on the stem; leathery; short-stalked; oblong to elliptic, mostly 1–3.5 cm long, narrowed at the base, rounded or acute at the tip; margins smooth or with small teeth, rolling slightly toward the undersurface; upper surface dark green and scurfy with small, light-colored scales, lower surface paler and scurfy.

Flowers: Bent to the lower side of the stem from the axils of upper leaves, forming arching, one-sided, leafy clusters at the ends of the branches **(a)**; corolla small, 5–7 mm, white, bell- or urn-shaped, with 5 recurving lobes, 10 stamens.

Fruit: Small, many-seeded capsule **(b)**, 3–4 mm across, splitting into 5 valves; empty capsules remain on the plant after the seeds are shed.

Phenology: Flowers bloom from mid-May to late June; the seeds mature and disperse in the fall.

Chimaphila umbellata (L.) Bart.
Pyrolaceae (Wintergreen Family)

Indicator Value/Significance to Forest Management

Pipsissewa is a shade-tolerant/intolerant dwarf shrub that is a good indicator of acidic, nutrient poor, well to excessively drained, moisture deficient soils with mor humus forms. These soils are usually coarse, sandy to loamy textured, and are found on water-shedding sites. Pipsissewa occurs in montane boreal, temperate, and cool-mesothermal climatic regimes. In British Columbia, its frequency of occurrence decreases with increasing elevation and precipitation, and increases with continentality. In white pine stands in the Great Lakes–St. Lawrence Forest

	Poor	Medium	Rich
Wet			
Moist			
Fresh			
Dry	▓		

Region, this species is characteristic of podzolized soils with iron pan formation, mor humus forms, and a low rate of organic matter decomposition. Pipsissewa has the same indicator values as poverty grass (*Danthonia spicata* [L.] Beauv.) and, in upland pine and black spruce stands, is often associated with stair-step moss, as well as other species of the wintergreen and heath families.

Distribution and Habitat

Distribution: Two varieties are recognized in Canada: variety *occidentalis* (Rydb.) Blake, from British Columbia to western James Bay, Ontario, with local occurrences in Alberta, Saskatchewan, and Manitoba; variety *cisatlantica* Blake, from eastern Manitoba to Nova Scotia and the southwestern tip of Newfoundland. Variety *occidentalis* is designated a rare species in Saskatchewan; in the United States, it is rare in Nevada and endangered in South Dakota; variety *cisatlantica* is rare on the island of Newfoundland.

Habitat: Moist, open or dense, coniferous forests in British Columbia; dry, sandy or rocky, pine and black spruce forests and clearings in eastern portions of the range.

Pipsissewa • Prince's Pine
Chimaphile à ombelle

Description

General: Dwarf woodland evergreen shrub with erect, leafy stems arising from a creeping rhizome, up to 30 cm tall.

Leaves: In several whorls or clusters along the stem; thick and leathery; oval, widest near the tip, 3–7 cm long, 1–2.2 cm wide, sharply toothed towards the tip; dark green, lustrous. In comparison to the eastern variety *cisatlantica*, the western variety *occidentalis* is slightly coarser, with leaves to 9 cm long.

Flowers: In terminal clusters of 4–8 flowers; corolla white or pink, 10–15 mm across, with 5 petals.

Fruit: Erect, persistent capsule, 5–6 mm across (6–7.5 mm across in western variety *occidentalis*); splitting apically; seeds numerous, light brown, with "tails" at each end.

Phenology: Flowers bloom between June and August; the fruit matures in August and September.

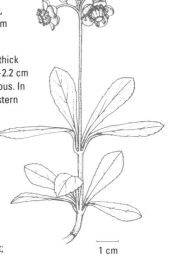

1 cm

Notes The rhizomes and leaves of pipsissewa are high in vitamin C and salicin, a natural painkiller, and can be either eaten raw or boiled into a refreshing drink. The leaves, which were once brewed as a tea by both aboriginal peoples and early pioneers, are now used as an ingredient in commercial root beer. Pipsissewa also has medicinal value as an antibiotic and is used in the manufacture of some modern medicines. Horticulturally the plant is attractive but difficult to transplant.

Comptonia peregrina (L.) Coult.
Myricaceae (Bayberry Family)

Indicator Value/Significance to Forest Management

Sweet-fern is a shade-intolerant, oxylophytic shrub that is a good indicator of dry, sandy, nutrient poor soils. It occurs in sunny, open habitats such as clearings, pastures, and open woodlands. Sweet-fern is apparently absent on limestone and dolomite outcrops; where it does occur in limestone areas (e.g., south-ern Ontario), it is associated with localized acidic, surficial deposits. The root nodules of sweet-fern fix atmospheric nitrogen, accounting for its ability to colonize sterile soils. The seeds are long-lived and may remain viable in the soil for 70 years.

Sweet-fern quickly invades burned areas, producing extensive, low shrub colonies that protect the soil from erosion and provide wildlife cover. The species also has great aesthetic value and provides visual relief to burn-scarred landscapes.

Sweet-fern is the alternate host for a blister rust that infects jack pine (*Pinus banksiana* Lamb.). Extracts of its foliage and roots inhibit survival, but not germination or growth, of red pine (*P. resinosa* Ait.) seedlings.

Distribution and Habitat

Distribution: Northwestern Ontario, east to Nova Scotia; rare or absent in areas underlain by limestone.

Habitat: Open sandy soils and dry barrens in woodlands, clearings, and pastures.

Sweet-fern
Comptonie voyageuse

Description

General: Much-branched, low, deciduous shrub, less than 1.5 m tall, with fragrant foliage, fruit, and twigs; twigs hairy.

Leaves: Opposite; linear-lanceolate, 6–12 cm long; margins deeply pinnately lobed; dark green above, pale below; may be hairy on one or both surfaces, dotted with resin glands; with pungent, spicy odor when crushed.

Flowers: Sexes are separate on the same plant; male catkins clustered, cylindric, 1–3 cm long, nodding; female catkins bur-like and terminal.

Fruit: Ellipsoid-shaped nutlets, blunt, 3–5 mm long; whole fruit bur-like, 1–2 cm across.

Phenology: Catkins fully expanded by the end of May in Ontario and Nova Scotia, and between mid-May and mid-June in Quebec; the fruit, with mature seeds, forms between early July and mid-August in Ontario and Quebec, and between mid-July and the end of September in Nova Scotia.

Synonym: *Myrica asplenifolia* of various reports, not L.

1 cm

1 cm

Notes   Sweet-fern can present a weed problem in hillside pastures, old fields, and open woods. In New Brunswick, it generally occurs in abandoned pastures and areas cleared of forest; it is a serious weed in commercial lowbush blueberry fields. The species is wind-pollinated, shedding large amounts of pollen, and is therefore considered to constitute a hay fever risk.

Cornus stolonifera Michx.
Cornaceae (Dogwood Family)

Indicator Value/Significance to Forest Management

Red-osier dogwood is a good indicator of nutrient medium, imperfectly to poorly drained, moist to wet soils, with some minor occurrences on drier soil conditions. These soils often support the development of moder and mull humus forms under boreal, temperate, and cool-mesothermal climatic regimes. This species is found on water-receiving sites (floodplains, alluvial flats) where it exhibits a tolerance for fluctuating groundwater levels. In mountainous regions, its frequency of occurrence decreases with increasing elevation. On wet sites, it is less selec-

tive with respect to soil nitrogen conditions. In the prairie provinces, red-osier dogwood is the primary tall shrub species under aspen, balsam poplar, and white spruce. In wetland habitats in the southern part of the Boreal Forest Region in Ontario, this species is associated with hardwood swamps on alluvial sites having neutral to slightly basic, nutrient rich, silt and clay-textured soils.

Red-osier dogwood can be a significant competitor of coniferous trees on wet, shrub dominated sites where it can regenerate and grow vigorously enough to hinder natural regeneration and growth of shade-intolerant conifer species. These sites are often very productive for crop tree growth.

Distribution and Habitat

Distribution: Throughout boreal and temperate North America, from Yukon and western Northwest Territories, British Columbia, east to Labrador and Newfoundland.

Habitat: Moist and wet habitats including thickets, margins of wetlands, rivers, lakes, and other low-lying areas, as well as in disturbed areas along roadsides and waste lands.

Red-Osier Dogwood
Hart rouge

Description

General: Stoloniferous deciduous shrub, mostly 1–3 m tall, with loosely spreading, purplish-red branches, often forming extensive thickets; lower branches often lie on the ground and root at the nodes; in winter, the bright red branches are very conspicuous.

Leaves: Opposite; elliptic to broadly oval, pointed and tapered at the tip, rounded at the base, 5–12 cm long; margins smooth; dark green above, finely soft-hairy and whitened below; with 5–7 pairs of sub-parallel veins curving inwards along the leaf margin towards the tip.

Flowers: Numerous, in open, flat-topped, terminal clusters, up to 5 cm across; individual flowers about 8 mm across, with 4 white petals.

Fruit: White, berry-like drupe, about 6 mm across, containing a somewhat flattened, 2-seeded stone.

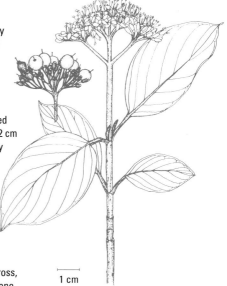

1 cm

Phenology: Flowers bloom between May and June in the northeastern United States and in June and July in Alaska; the fruit ripens from July to September; second flushes of bloom are common in late summer in the northeastern United States.

Synonym: *Cornus sericea* L.

Notes The flexible, young branches (osiers) are used by aboriginal peoples for basket-weaving; the red bark has also been used as a smoking mixture ingredient and to make a red dye. This species is an important summer and winter food source for wildlife, particularly deer, moose, and birds. The fruits and new shoots are the most utilized browse parts of the plant in summer, while the twigs are consumed in winter. It has been shown that browsing increases sprout density. This species is used for forage by bear, beaver, snowshoe hare, and many other mammals. Red-osier dogwood also provides nesting habitat for many species of birds.

Corylus cornuta Marsh.
Betulaceae (Birch Family)

Indicator Value/Significance to Forest Management

Beaked hazel is a shade-tolerant/intolerant shrub that is an indicator of basic, calcium rich soils having high levels of available nitrogen and a fresh soil moisture regime. Soil conditions supporting beaked hazel are typically associated with water-shedding sites and are characterized by moder and mull humus forms developed under cool-temperate and cool-mesothermal climatic regimes. In British Columbia, the frequency of occurrence of beaked hazel decreases with increasing latitude and precipitation, and increases with increasing continentality.

Associated species with similar indicator values include mountain maple (*Acer spicatum* Lam.), red baneberry, sweet-scented bedstraw, shining clubmoss, and bristly black currant. Beaked hazel grows vigorously on well-aerated loamy sands, sandy loams, and loams, favoring soils that are moist, but well drained, rich in calcium and nitrogen, and slightly acidic (pH 5.3–6.1). It does poorly in very acidic and near-neutral soils and in wet, poorly aerated soils. It has, however, a high tolerance for flooding. As an understory species it grows well under an open canopy of red or jack pine, aspen or aspen–birch, and mixed conifer–hardwood forests, but dense shade inhibits growth and diminishes seed production. It is common in young, seral, broadleaved forests.

Beaked hazel is a very aggressive competitor and a major deterrent to conifer regeneration. The densely layered growth of beaked hazel shades out conifers and other species, and its extensive, shallow root system causes considerable competition for soil moisture and nutrients. Beaked hazel is well adapted to open conditions and will rapidly colonize a site after harvesting or other disturbance, thus minimizing soil erosion; however, it is difficult to eradicate with site preparation. On the other hand, rapid recycling of nutrients by beaked hazel may benefit crop species.

Distribution and Habitat

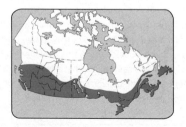

Distribution: British Columbia, east to Newfoundland, but not found in northern regions and Labrador.

Habitat: Rich thickets and clearings, streambanks and shorelines, occurring as an understory shrub in open forests.

Beaked Hazel
Noisetier à long bec

Description

General: Small to medium-sized deciduous shrub, up to 3 m tall, often forming dense thickets; older twigs may be rough or smooth, dark brown or gray, often appearing striped.

Leaves: Alternate; broadly oval to obovate in shape, rounded or heart-shaped at the base, tapering to a point at the tip, 5–10 cm long; margins irregularly and coarsely double-toothed; hairy on the undersurface.

Flowers: Sexes are separate but on the same plant; male catkins about 5 cm long at anthesis, pendulous, greenish-yellow, appearing before the leaves; female flowers in small clusters, concealed in the buds except for protruding crimson stigmas.

Fruit: Rounded, pale brown, hard-shelled nut enclosed in a bristly husk with an elongated beak **(a)**; solitary or clustered in groups of 2 or 3.

Phenology: Flowers are formed on 1-year-old twigs late in the summer and emerge before the leaves the following spring; generally flowering in late April to early June; the fruit ripens in late summer or early fall.

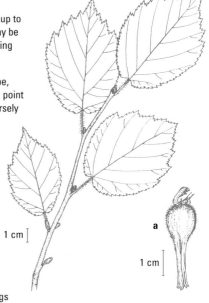

1 cm

a

1 cm

Notes Beaked hazel is an important winter browse species for moose and deer. The hazelnuts, which are flavorful and nutritious, are consumed in large quantities by many species of small mammals and birds. The dense thickets produced by this species provide cover for woodcock and grouse. Aboriginal peoples have traditionally used the nut oil in food preparations and as a treatment for toothaches. The nuts can be eaten raw, slightly roasted, or crushed into a meal.

Dirca palustris L.
Thymelaeaceae (Mezereum Family)

Indicator Value/Significance to Forest Management

Leatherwood is a shade-tolerant shrub that is a good indicator, over its range, of fresh, nutrient rich soils with mull humus forms. It occurs on water-receiving sites in sugar maple and basswood–sugar maple stands in the Great Lakes–

	Poor	Medium	Rich
Wet			
Moist			
Fresh			▓
Dry			

St. Lawrence Forest Region. It is strongly associated with false spikenard, hairy Solomon's-seal (*Polygonatum pubescens* [Willd.] Pursh), and Selkirk's violet (*Viola selkirkii* Pursh ex J. Goldie).

Distribution and Habitat

Distribution: Northern Ontario, east through the deciduous forests of Quebec, New Brunswick, and Nova Scotia. Leatherwood has been designated as a rare species in Nova Scotia; in the United States, it is rare in Florida, Illinois, Louisiana, and Oklahoma, endangered in Georgia, and threatened in Maine.

Habitat: Rich, moist, deciduous or mixed forests.

Leatherwood • Wicopy
Dirca des marais

Description

General: Freely branched, single-stemmed deciduous shrub,
1–2 m tall, with jointed twigs and very tough, leatherlike bark;
bearing lateral clusters of 2–4 pale yellow flowers.

Leaves: Alternate; broadly ovate to obovate,
rounded or acute at the tip, cuneate at the base,
5–8 cm long; on very short stalks.

Flowers: Sepals petal-like, light yellow, tubular,
truncate with wavy margins.

Fruit: Ellipsoid drupe about 8 mm long.

Phenology: Flowers bloom in early spring
before the leaves appear.

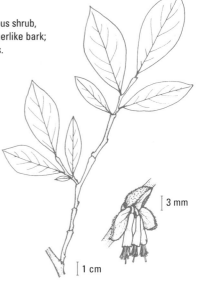

3 mm

1 cm

Notes   Some people develop a severe irritation and blistering of the skin after handling
the bark of this plant.

Epigaea repens L.
Ericaceae (Heath Family)

Indicator Value/Significance to Forest Management

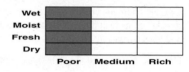

Mayflower is a shade-tolerant/intolerant, low, trailing shrub that is a good indicator of acidic, sandy to coarse loamy soils with low levels of available nitrogen. It occurs on water-shedding and water-receiving sites on soils with a broad range of moisture conditions, but mostly it is found on dry sites. In the western part of the Great Lakes–St. Lawrence Forest Region, mayflower is characteristic of sites with dry, colloid poor, sandy soils capable of supporting pure jack pine stands. In the Acadian Forest Region and in the eastern extreme of the Boreal Forest Region in Newfoundland, it occurs on a wider spectrum of soil moisture regimes, but the soils are similar in other characteristics to those elsewhere in its range.

	Poor	Medium	Rich
Wet	■		
Moist	■		
Fresh	■		
Dry	■		

Distribution and Habitat

Distribution: Southern Manitoba, east to Newfoundland.

Habitat: In the western part of its range, dry to fresh, sandy and coarse loamy soils, usually under pine and black spruce; on the east coast, more frequently associated with coniferous woods, boggy barrens, serpentine slopes, limestone ledges, and mountain tops.

Mayflower • Trailing Arbutus
Épigée rampante

Description

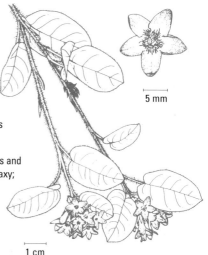

5 mm

General: Prostrate, trailing, evergreen shrub with green to reddish-brown, hairy branches; usually forming patches.

Leaves: Alternate; slightly leathery; oval, blunt-tipped, rounded or heart-shaped at the base, 2.5–7 cm long; both upper and lower surfaces shiny and hairy, rough to the touch; margins and stalk hairy.

Flowers: In small crowded clusters in the leaf axils and at the ends of branches; pink or white, fragrant, waxy; corolla tube-shaped, hairy inside, with the end expanded into 5 flat lobes, 1.5 cm across.

Fruit: Dry, 5-valved, globular capsule containing many small seeds.

1 cm

Phenology: Flowers bloom from mid-May to late June; the seeds mature in August.

Notes | The flower petals are spicy, slightly acidic, and edible.

Gaultheria shallon Pursh
Ericaceae (Heath Family)

Indicator Value/Significance to Forest Management

Salal is a shade-tolerant/intolerant shrub that is an indicator of acidic, nutrient poor soils characterized by mor humus forms. It prefers dry to fresh, non-seepage soils that are deep enough to support tree growth, and is associated with water-shedding sites in hypermaritime to maritime, cool-mesothermal climates. Its frequency of occurrence decreases with increasing elevation and continentality. This species is often dominant in open-canopy, coniferous forests, as well as in cutovers with intact forest floors, where it forms extensive thickets. On nutrient

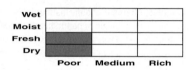

rich sites, it is restricted to decaying coniferous wood. On moist or wet sites, it is found only on micro-topographic prominences where soils are locally drier. Salal is absent or sporadic in the shaded understory of immature, closed-canopy stands.

Salal is a common and serious competitor of coniferous tree species in low-elevation coastal British Columbia, particularly on mesic and drier sites. It is capable of ecologically dominating a site, and is most serious as a competitor in the early stages of conifer stand development. Salal forms extensive horizontal root systems in the uppermost soil layers. Both the roots and foliage of salal are decay resistant. Thus, prolific development of salal on a forest site reduces the availability of soil water for other species and also retards the decomposition of forest floor organic matter. These conditions hinder the growth of crop species, and forest regeneration in general, particularly on moisture deficient sites.

Distribution and Habitat

Distribution: Coastal British Columbia, with an isolated population in the southeastern interior of the province.

Habitat: Mainly coniferous forests, thickets, rocky cliffs, ravines, and exposed shores.

Salal
Salal

Description

General: Partially prostrate to erect, freely branched evergreen shrub, with hairy stems, to 2.5 m tall; sometimes forming impenetrable thickets.

Leaves: Alternate; smooth, shiny, leathery; ovate to ovate-elliptic, rounded to heart-shaped at the base; on short stalks.

Flowers: Clustered in terminal and axillary one-sided racemes of up to 15 flowers; corolla white or pink, glandular, urn-shaped, with 5 triangular-shaped lobes, each about one-third the length of the corolla.

Fruit: A capsule; when ripe, enclosed by the calyx, which thickens and becomes fleshy, appearing berry-like; nearly black; containing many small seeds.

Phenology: Flowering is variable and can occur any time between March and July, usually occurring from May to June in Alaska and between early June and July in southern British Columbia; the fruits ripen between August and October, remaining on the stem until December.

1 cm

Notes   Salal is an important source of food for wildlife, particularly for deer (which use it year-round), elk, and a variety of small mammal and bird species; stems, leaves, blossoms, and fruit are consumed. Ripe salal berries are edible and widely used by aboriginal peoples on the west coast of British Columbia. This shrub has high ornamental value, but tends to be invasive.

Juniperus communis L.
Cupressaceae (Cypress Family)

Indicator Value/Significance to Forest Management

Common juniper is a shade-intolerant shrub that is an indicator of nutrient poor and nutrient medium, dry to very dry soils that are often associated with disturbed sites. It is found on acidic soils as well as on chalk and limestone, but becomes chlorotic on alkaline sites. It occurs sporadically on water-shedding sites in early-seral communities, on shallow soils over bedrock, in dry open woods, and in clearings. In British Columbia, its frequency of occurrence increases with increasing latitude and continentality. On Vancouver Island, dense patches of com-

mon juniper, often in association with bearberry, indicate habitats that are too dry, and soils too shallow, to support tree growth. In the Boreal Forest Region, this species shows high regional presence values for white spruce–balsam fir stands between northern British Columbia and Lake Winnipeg. In wet habitats in the Northern Clay Section of the Boreal Forest Region in northern Ontario, it is a good indicator of fen conditions. In the eastern Great Lakes–St. Lawrence and Acadian Forest Regions, common juniper is associated with dry shallow soils among rock outcrops.

Distribution and Habitat

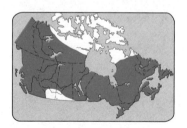

Distribution: Transcontinental in North America, across most of Canada.

Habitat: Dry woods and old fields, rocky hillsides, peatlands, heaths, and other open habitats.

Common Juniper
Genévrier commun

Description

General: Prostrate or spreading, evergreen shrub (rarely arborescent), commonly forming low, open thickets, up to 1.5 m tall; young stems smooth, greenish and ridged; older stems brown, with scaly bark.

Leaves: Needle-like; awl-shaped, with a sharp-pointed tip, 5–20 mm long **(a)**; arranged in whorls of 3; upper surface (facing the stem) with a white stripe down the middle, bordered by green margins; lower surface green and shiny.

Cones: In the leaf axils, male and female cones sometimes on separate plants; male cones catkin-like, 2–4 mm long; immature female cones oval-shaped, about 1 mm long, consisting of 3–8 minute scales. Mature female cones fleshy, aromatic, berry-like, blue to black with a whitish-blue bloom, about 6 mm across, containing 1–3 seeds; persistent on the plant over a period of 2–3 years; seeds dispersed by birds and small mammals that eat the cones and excrete the seeds.

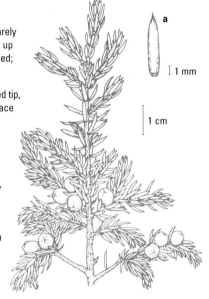

a

1 mm

1 cm

Phenology: Pollination occurs in April and May; female cones mature in the second or third season after fertilization.

Synonym: *Juniperus sibirica* Burgsd.

> *Notes* The "berries" of common juniper are used to flavor gin and other cordials. Oils distilled from the wood are used in perfumery and, sometimes, medicinally. The "berries" are a diuretic, a stimulant, and a carminative (easing griping pain and expelling flatulence). They are eaten in winter by many species of mammals and birds, and the foliage is browsed by deer and sheep when other food sources are scarce. Common juniper has high value as an ornamental shrub, and its many varieties are widely used for landscaping.

Kalmia angustifolia L.
Ericaceae (Heath Family)

Indicator Value/Significance to Forest Management

Sheep-laurel is a shade-tolerant/intolerant shrub occurring across a wide range of nutritional and soil moisture conditions. It is most commonly associated with nutrient poor soils, but can be found on rich sites as well.

In the eastern part of the Boreal Forest Region, sheep-laurel is characteristically present in black spruce–jack pine stands, and absent or infrequent in white spruce–balsam fir stands. In Ontario, this species is indicative of oligotrophic, shrub rich,

	Poor	Medium	Rich
Wet			
Moist			
Fresh			
Dry			

treed bogs with undecomposed peat and a near-surface water table. In wooded habitats, it is often associated with sweet-fern and low sweet blueberry (*Vaccinium angustifolium* Ait.).

Sheep-laurel can constitute a serious forest management problem. Even sparse populations of sheep-laurel under a forest canopy can quickly become ecologically dominant on a site if the forest cover is removed through cutting or fire. Once dominant on a site it is very difficult to eradicate. Some research indicates that this species is able to maintain its dominance by producing allelopathic leaf exudates which inhibit seed germination and primary root development of seedlings of other species. Its slowly decomposing, organic acid rich litter results in nitrogen poor humus and lower soil pH levels. These soil changes can cause iron pan formation and subsequent conversion of well-drained sites to wet sites as drainage becomes increasingly impeded and water tables rise.

Distribution and Habitat

Distribution: Southern James Bay in northern Ontario, east to central and southern Labrador and Newfoundland.

Habitat: Dry or wet, sterile, acidic soils in bogs, swamps, heaths, and forested areas.

Sheep-Laurel
Kalmia à feuilles étroites

Description

General: Much-branched, evergreen shrub, up to
1 m tall, arising from creeping rhizomes; often forming
extensive colonies; stem smooth, reddish-brown.

Leaves: Opposite or in whorls of 3; on short
stalks; narrowly to broadly oblong or elliptic,
2–5 cm long, tip blunt to pointed; leathery, olive-
green and shiny above, pale green and dull below;
margins smooth.

Flowers: Several in showy clusters **(a)** along the
stems at the base of new growth; corolla rose-
pink (rarely white), bowl-shaped, about 1.2 cm
across; stamens 10, caught in tiny pockets on
the corolla and springing out when the flower
is touched.

Fruit: Dry, flattened, globular, 5-part capsule **(b)**, about 4 mm across, containing
numerous small seeds.

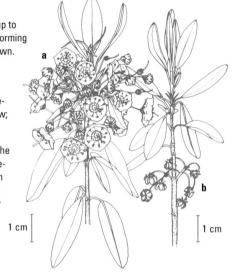

1 cm

1 cm

Phenology: Flowers bloom from late June to early August; the seeds ripen
in the fall but often remain in the capsules on the plant throughout the winter.

Notes   Sheep-laurel contains a toxic substance known as andromedotoxin that has
caused poisoning and death in cattle, sheep, goats, and horses on ingestion. It is also poisonous to humans, but it is unlikely anyone would eat the plant under normal conditions as
the leaves are tough and bitter. Honey made by bees that have worked the flowers of sheep-
laurel may also be poisonous to humans.

Kalmia polifolia Wangenh.
Ericaceae (Heath Family)

Indicator Value/Significance to Forest Management

Bog-laurel is a shade-intolerant, oxylophytic shrub that is an indicator of nutrient poor, wet to very wet soils. It is found in scattered occurrences in non-forested, semi-terrestrial communities on water-collecting peatland sites under tundra and boreal climatic regimes. In British Columbia, its frequency of occurrence increases with increasing latitude and continentality. In the eastern Boreal Forest Region, bog-laurel occurs sporadically in black spruce stands, but is absent or infrequent in white spruce–balsam fir stands. In the southern section of the Boreal

	Poor	Medium	Rich
Wet	■		
Moist			
Fresh			
Dry			

Forest Region in Ontario, this species is indicative of very oligotrophic, low shrub and graminoid rich, treed fens with poorly decomposed peat and surface-level water tables. Bog-laurel is often associated with leatherleaf, Labrador-tea, rhodora, small cranberry, and several species of moss genus *Sphagnum*.

Distribution and Habitat

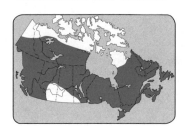

Distribution: Yukon and British Columbia, east to Labrador and Newfoundland.

Habitat: Wet, organic soils; in bogs, fens, black spruce peatlands, and along lakeshores.

Bog-Laurel
Kalmia à feuilles d'andromède

Description

General: Low, few- to much-branched, slender, evergreen shrub, up to 40 cm tall; stems smooth and 2-ridged.

Leaves: Opposite; 1.5–3 cm long; without stalks; linear to narrowly elliptic, usually blunt at the tip; leathery, shiny, dark-green above **(a)**, whitened with a prominent midvein below **(b)**; margins rolling towards the undersurface.

Flowers: Few, in terminal clusters; on long, slender stalks; corolla deep pink, bowl-shaped, 5-lobed, about 1.3 cm across; stamens 10, caught in tiny pockets on the corolla and springing out when the flower is touched.

Fruit: Oval, erect, red, 5-part capsule, about 5 mm long, containing many small seeds.

Phenology: Flowers bloom in June; the seeds ripen in August.

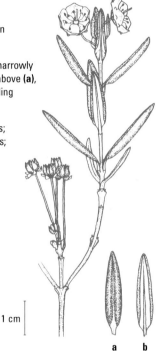

1 cm

a   b

Notes   Bog-laurel contains the same toxic compound as sheep-laurel, but it is seldom encountered by livestock because of its mainly wetland habitat.

Ledum decumbens (Ait.) Lodd.
Ericaceae (Heath Family)

Indicator Value/Significance to Forest Management

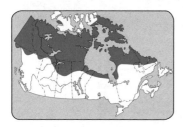

Northern Labrador-tea is a shade-intolerant, oxylophytic dwarf shrub that is an indicator of nutrient poor soils having a dry soil moisture regime. Northern Labrador-tea is often associated with permafrost peat plateaus, and typically occurs on northern heaths, dry sunny ledges, and rocky places under subarctic and arctic climatic regimes.

	Poor	Medium	Rich
Wet			
Moist			
Fresh			
Dry	■		

Distribution and Habitat

Distribution: Yukon, Northwest Territories, northern British Columbia, Saskatchewan, Ontario, Quebec, and Labrador. Northern Labrador-tea has been designated as a rare species in British Columbia and Ontario.

Habitat: Dry hills and rocky barrens; moist, shrub and moss–lichen heaths; sunny cliffs and ledges.

Northern Labrador-Tea • Dwarf Labrador-Tea
Lédon décombant

Description

General: Prostrate, decumbent or ascending, dwarf evergreen shrub, to 50 cm tall; similar in appearance to Labrador-tea, but smaller.

Leaves: Alternate; narrow, linear, 1–2.5 cm long, 2–3 mm wide **(a)**; margins rolling strongly towards the undersurface; leathery, dark green and wrinkled above, densely hairy below with rust-colored hairs.

Flowers: In terminal clusters **(b)** about 3 cm across; corolla white, deeply 5-lobed and appearing separate, with 10 stamens.

Fruit: Dry, slender capsules on arching stalks **(c)**; about 3–4 mm long; otherwise similar to Labrador-tea.

Phenology: Flowers bloom from June to August; the seeds mature in the fall.

Synonyms: *Ledum palustre* L. ssp. *decumbens* (Ait.) Hult.; *L. palustre* L. var. *decumbens* Ait.

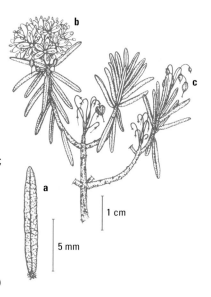

1 cm

5 mm

Notes Like Labrador-tea, the foliage of northern Labrador-tea contains a toxic compound which, if consumed in large enough quantities, may cause cramps and paralysis.

Ledum groenlandicum Oeder
Ericaceae (Heath Family)

Indicator Value/Significance to Forest Management

Labrador-tea is a shade-intolerant, oxylophytic low shrub that is a moderate indicator of soils with moist to wet moisture regimes, and poor nutrient conditions. These soils are usually highly acidic and nitrogen poor and may be either organic or gleyed mineral soils, characterized by mor humus forms developed under boreal, cool-temperate, and cool-mesothermal climatic regimes. Labrador-tea typically occurs on water-collecting sites having stagnant water tables; it is common on peatlands in open and treed sphagnum dominated wetlands and in open-

	Poor	Medium	Rich
Wet	■		
Moist	■		
Fresh			
Dry			

canopy coniferous forests. In British Columbia its frequency of occurrence decreases with increasing temperature. Common associates include leatherleaf, bog-laurel, and several species of the moss genus *Sphagnum*. In west-central Alberta, white spruce (*Picea glauca* [Moench] Voss) productivity is lowered on sites with abundant Labrador-tea. Labrador-tea shows a very high regional presence value for black spruce stands throughout the Boreal Forest Region. In the southern part of the Boreal Forest Region of Ontario, this species is indicative of oligotrophic, shrub rich, treed bogs with undecomposed peat and a near-surface water table.

Labrador-tea may compete with coniferous species for nitrogen and phosphorus uptake. It has a more efficient uptake capacity and, with a shallower root system, can avail itself of these nutrients earlier in the spring than can the later developing conifers. Labrador-tea is also the alternate host of some needle rusts (*Chrysomyxa* spp.) which can cause moderate to heavy defoliation of spruce. There is some evidence that this species is allelopathic.

Distribution and Habitat

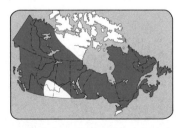

Distribution: Yukon, northern and eastern British Columbia, east to Labrador and Newfoundland; absent only in the far north, in the southern prairies of Alberta and Saskatchewan, and in southwestern Ontario.

Habitat: A broad range of soil/site conditions in bogs, fens, wet and dry heaths, and on upland sites with poor drainage.

Labrador-Tea
Lédon du Groenland

Description

General: Erect, freely branching, evergreen shrub, up to 1 m tall; old stems reddish-brown to gray; new twigs densely covered with brown hairs.

Leaves: Alternate; usually crowded at the tips of the branches; narrowly elliptic with a rounded tip, 1.5–5 cm long, 4–12 mm wide **(a)**; margins smooth, rolling strongly towards the undersurface; thick and leathery; upper surface dull, dark green and deeply veined; lower surface with dense, rusty, mat-like hairs; persisting on the stem for 3 or more years.

Flowers: In terminal, roundish clusters **(b)** on the upper branches, 2–5 cm across; corolla white, deeply 5-lobed, about 1 cm across; 5–7 stamens, longer than the corolla-lobes.

Fruit: Dry, slender, pendant capsules on arching stalks **(c)**; about 6 mm long, splitting into 5 parts upwards from the base; with persistent styles.

Phenology: Flowers bloom from early June to mid-July; the seeds ripen in the fall; capsules are often persistent on the plants for several months.

Notes   Labrador-tea is an important browse species for woodland caribou from the time that deciduous shrubs lose their leaves in the fall until green sedges appear in the spring. Numerous aboriginal groups across Canada, as well as European explorers and settlers, have used the aromatic leaves of this shrub to make a medicinal tea. However, the leaves contain a toxic compound which, in high enough dosage, can cause cramps and paralysis. A brown dye can be extracted from the leaves. Labrador-tea has the ability to concentrate zinc and copper, and thus has value in geobotanical studies.

Lonicera involucrata (Richards.) Banks
Caprifoliaceae (Honeysuckle Family)

Indicator Value/Significance to Forest Management

Bracted honeysuckle is a shade-tolerant/intolerant, nitrophytic shrub that is a good indicator of nutrient rich, moist to wet soils. It commonly occurs on water-receiving (alluvial, floodplain, seepage, streambank) and water-collecting (rich wetlands) sites, where it is scattered to plentiful in open and deciduous forest habitats. It shows tolerance for fluctuating ground-water levels. It occurs on either organic or mineral soils, which develop moder and mull humus forms under boreal, temperate, and cool-mesothermal climates. In British Columbia, this species is asso-

	Poor	Medium	Rich
Wet			■
Moist			
Fresh			
Dry			

ciated with thimbleberry, red-osier dogwood, and Pacific crabapple (*Malus fusca* [Raf.] Schneider) in coastal habitats, and with salmonberry, red osier dogwood, and cow-parsnip (*Heracleum lanatum* Michx.) in the interior. Bracted honeysuckle is associated with black spruce stands in northern Alberta and Saskatchewan, but is absent or infrequent in white spruce–balsam fir stands in the Boreal Forest Region. In northern Ontario it shows a preference for calcareous soils.

Bracted honeysuckle tends to persist on cutover sites, where it may pose a problem for natural regeneration and growth of shade-intolerant coniferous species. However, it is not considered a serious threat to coniferous tree regeneration and growth.

Distribution and Habitat

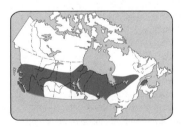

Distribution: Southern and central British Columbia, east through central Alberta, Saskatchewan and Manitoba, northern Ontario, and west-central Quebec, also the Gaspé Peninsula.

Habitat: Cool, moist to wet, swampy woods and thickets, and along streambanks and lakeshores in wooded and open areas; on either mineral or organic soils, preferring calcareous substrates.

Bracted Honeysuckle • Black Twinberry
Chèvrefeuille involucré

Description

General: Upright deciduous shrub with erect, ascending branches, 1–3 m tall; young stems smooth, greenish to purplish; older stems slightly 4-sided; the squarish stems and pointed leaves distinguish this species from non-flowering individuals of other honeysuckles.

Leaves: Opposite; stalks about 1 cm long; elliptic to ovate or obovate, with an abruptly pointed tip and rounded to tapering base; dark green and nearly smooth above, paler and hairy below; margins fringed with white hairs.

Flowers: In pairs at the ends of long stalks arising from the leaf axils; each pair of flowers subtended by 2 large, round, sharp-tipped, green to purple bracts, and 2 smaller but similar bracteoles; corolla narrowly tubular, with straight or barely spreading, rounded lobes; the large floral bracts are diagnostic for this species.

1 cm

1 cm

Fruit: A pair of shiny, purple-black berries, 6–9 mm across, subtended by the enlarged bracts and bracteoles.

Phenology: Flowers bloom from July to September in Ontario, and between March or April and August in British Columbia, depending partly on elevation; the fruit matures between July or August and early fall.

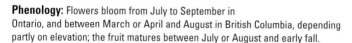

Notes   Bracted honeysuckle provides habitat and food for wildlife. It is used as winter browse by elk and moose and provides summer forage for birds, bears, and other mammals. Snowshoe hares in Alberta, however, tend to avoid eating this plant. The berries are considered to be toxic to humans and ingestion may cause illness and vomiting.

Mahonia aquifolium (Pursh) Nutt.
Berberidaceae (Barberry Family)

Indicator Value/Significance to Forest Management

Tall Oregon-grape is a shade-tolerant/intolerant shrub that is a good indicator of nutrient medium, moisture deficient soils with thin moder and mull humus forms. This species occurs predominantly in continental, cool-temperate and cool, semi-arid climates where it is commonly found in open-canopy Douglas-fir forests in the coast–interior ecotone of British Columbia. It is sporadic in summer-dry, mesothermal climates, with its frequency of occurrence generally increasing with increasing summer drought and continentality. Species often associated with tall Oregon-grape are couch-grass (*Agropyron repens* [L.] Beauv.), purple reedgrass (*Calamagrostis rubescens* Buckley), and electrified cat's tail moss (*Rhytidiadelphus triquetrus* [Hedw.] Warnst.).

Distribution and Habitat

Distribution: Southern British Columbia and southwestern Alberta; introduced in southern Ontario and southwestern Quebec.

Habitat: Open woods, sagebrush covered hills and slopes to 1200 m elevation.

Tall Oregon-Grape
Mahonia à feuilles de houx

Description

General: Low evergreen shrub, up to 2 m tall, stiffly erect to trailing and stoloniferous; with leathery leaves and yellowish inner bark and wood.

Leaves: Alternate; upper surface shiny, lower surface shiny to dull; pinnately compound, with 5–9 leaflets; leaflets twice as long as wide or more, margins spiny.

Flowers: Few to many in clusters; corolla yellow; 6 petals and 6 sepals, 3 bracts below the sepals.

Fruit: Berries borne on long stalks; berries up to 14 mm across, blue with a white bloom, containing one to a few seeds.

Phenology: Flowers bloom between April and June.

Synonym: *Berberis aquifolium* Pursh

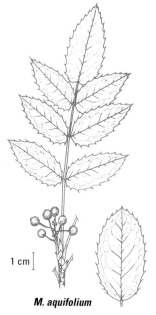

1 cm

M. aquifolium

M. repens
(leaflet)

Notes   A similar species, **holly-grape** (*Mahonia repens* Lindl.), also occurs in the high mountains of southern British Columbia and southwestern Alberta, on rocky ledges and in sparse coniferous forests. Its leaves have fewer leaflets, on average, than do those of tall Oregon-grape, and the leaflets have more teeth.

   The berries of tall Oregon-grape, although sour (better after frost), are edible and may be made into jellies and jams; they also make a grape-like juice when mixed with sugar. The shrub has been used medicinally by aboriginal peoples as a tonic and a blood purifier, as well as to treat psoriasis and sore throats. This shrub is considered a choice ornamental plant because of its habit, evergreen leaves, and attractive flowers and fruits.

Mahonia nervosa (Pursh) Nutt.
Berberidaceae (Barberry Family)

Indicator Value/Significance to Forest Management

Dull Oregon-grape is a shade-tolerant/intolerant shrub that is a moderate indicator of nutrient medium, fine to coarsely textured soils with moderately dry to fresh soil moisture regimes and thin, friable mor and moder humus forms. Its occurrence is scattered to abundant on water-shedding sites in the understory of open-canopy forests under maritime to submaritime, cool-mesothermal climates. It is persistent on cutover sites. It is characteristic of the Coast Forest Region, with its frequency of occurrence decreasing with increasing precipitation, elevation, and continentality. Associated species include salal, Oregon beaked moss, and sword fern.

Distribution and Habitat

Distribution: West of the Cascades Mountain Range in southwestern British Columbia.

Habitat: Open-canopy forests in the Coastal and Interior Wet Belts, to 1400 m elevation.

Dull Oregon-Grape
Mahonia à nervures saillantes

Description

General: Evergreen shrub up to 2 m tall, stiffly erect to trailing and stoloniferous; with leathery leaves and yellowish inner bark and wood.

Leaves: Alternate; upper surface shiny, lower surface shiny to dull; pinnately compound with 9–19 leaflets; leaflets mostly over 4 cm long; margins spiny.

Flowers: Few to many in clusters; corolla yellow; 6 petals and 6 sepals, 3 bracts below the sepals.

Fruit: Berries nearly sessile; berries up to 11 mm across, blue with a white bloom, containing one to several seeds.

Phenology: Flowers bloom from March to June, depending on the location.

Synonym: *Berberis nervosa* Pursh

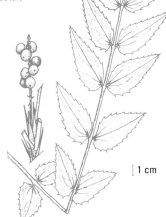

| 1 cm

Notes　　Non-fruiting individuals of this species can be differentiated from those of tall Oregon-grape on the basis of more numerous leaflets per compound leaf and the more or less palmate leaflet venation (leaflets of tall Oregon-grape are pinnately veined).

The berries of dull Oregon-grape are similar to those of tall Oregon-grape, and can be used to make juice, jellies, and jams. The shrub has been used medicinally by aboriginal peoples to treat a range of ailments, including liver and urinary problems, and venereal disease. The shrub is a choice ornamental plant due to its habit, evergreen foliage, and attractive flowers and fruits.

Menziesia ferruginea Sm.
Ericaceae (Heath Family)

Indicator Value/Significance to Forest Management

False azalea is a shade-tolerant/intolerant, oxylophytic shrub that is a moderate indicator of nutrient poor soils with moderately dry to fresh soil moisture regimes. It normally occurs in areas of high precipitation. In Alberta, this species is characteristic of late snowmelt areas high in the mountains. Soils on these sites develop mor humus forms under boreal, cool-temperate, and cool-mesothermal climatic regimes. False azalea is scattered to plentiful on water-shedding sites in the understory of coniferous forests. On nutrient rich sites, it is restricted to decaying conif-

	Poor	Medium	Rich
Wet			
Moist			
Fresh	▓		
Dry			

erous wood. Its frequency of occurrence tends to increase with increasing precipitation. Associated species include stair-step moss, lanky moss, the moss *Rhytidiopsis robusta* (Hedw.) Broth., and several species of *Vaccinium*.

False azalea is a member of an ericaceous shrub complex, also including white-flowered rhododendron and several *Vaccinium* spp., that is abundant on well-drained mesic sites in coastal British Columbia and in moist mountain areas in the interior. Although this species complex often dominates logged sites, its effects on regeneration and growth of coniferous crop species are not well known. This complex is considered to be a problem for regeneration only in the southern interior of the province. Regrowth of false azalea following cutting and scarification is slow, suggesting that conifer seedlings planted promptly following logging would not be seriously affected by this individual species.

Distribution and Habitat

Distribution: Southwestern Yukon, coastal and southern British Columbia, east to western Alberta.

Habitat: Common on moist slopes in mountain forests and shady woods.

False Azalea • Rustyleaf
Menziésie ferrugineuse

Description

General: Deciduous shrub, with erect to spreading branches, up to 2 m tall; older branches with loosely shredding bark; foliage and young twigs finely hairy with glandular hairs; often forming thickets.

Leaves: Alternate; short-stalked; thin, finely hairy, light green; oblong to elliptic, up to 6 cm long, tapering to the base and acute-tipped; margins smooth to wavy, with small bristly hairs.

Flowers: Flowers several, pendant on long stalks below the new year's growth; corolla yellowish-red, urn- to tube-shaped, up to 1 cm long, with 4–5 shallow lobes; calyx lobes and stalks glandular-hairy.

Fruit: Oval-shaped capsule up to 8 mm long.

Phenology: Flowers bloom from May to July, appearing with the leaves; the capsules mature in July or August.

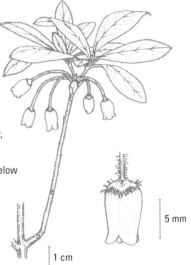

5 mm

1 cm

Notes   False azalea is seldom browsed and is generally considered unimportant to ungulates as a food source, although deer are known to consume it to a limited degree. Poisoning and death of sheep have been reported as a result of ingestion of this plant.

Nemopanthus mucronata (L.) Trel.
Aquifoliaceae (Holly Family)

Indicator Value/Significance to Forest Management

Mountain-holly is a shade-intolerant shrub characteristic of acidic, nutrient poor to medium, moist to wet, organic soils. It is found on water-collecting sites in marshes and bogs, often with scattered black spruce and larch. In the southern Boreal Forest Region in Ontario and in the eastern Great Lakes–St. Lawrence and Acadian Forest Regions of eastern Canada, mountain-holly is a pioneer invader of open bog communities and is indicative of oligotrophic, shrub rich, treed bogs with undecomposed peat and a near-surface water table. In

	Poor	Medium	Rich
Wet	▓	▓	
Moist	▓	▓	
Fresh			
Dry			

boreal Newfoundland, it is characteristic of nutrient poor soils over a wide range of moisture conditions, and is typically found in open, usually stunted, black spruce stands on wet sites surrounding bogs. On drier sites in this part of its range, mountain-holly is often sparse under balsam fir or balsam fir–black spruce, becoming abundant following clear-cutting, fire, or heavy insect infestation. It is often associated with sheep-laurel, wild-raisin (*Viburnum cassinoides* L.), American yew, goldthread, rhodora, and Labrador-tea.

Distribution and Habitat

Distribution: North-central Ontario, east to Newfoundland.

Habitat: Moist to wet habitats in thickets, bogs, swamps, and woods; in Newfoundland, exposed habitats such as coastal heaths.

Mountain-Holly
Némopanthe mucroné

Description

General: Medium-sized, much-branched deciduous shrub up to 3 m tall; twigs smooth, purplish-brown, either long and slender, with widely spaced leaves, or shorter and thicker, with leaves more crowded and appearing whorled.

Leaves: Alternate; oblong, with rounded to acute base and tip, often with a small point at the tip, 2.5–8 cm long; thin and smooth, bright green above, dull and paler below; margins smooth to irregularly toothed.

Flowers: Solitary or in clusters of up to 5, on slender stalks arising from the leaf axils; male and female flowers usually on separate plants; individual flowers small, 6 mm across, yellowish, with 4–5 petals.

Fruit: Purplish-red, berry-like drupe, about 6 mm across, containing 4 or 5 nutlets; borne on slightly divergent to pendant, slender stalks.

Phenology: Flowers bloom in late May or early June; the seeds ripen in August and September.

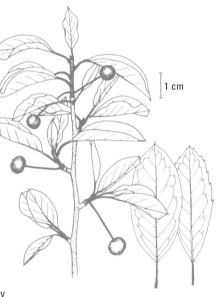

1 cm

Oplopanax horridus (Sm.) Miq.
Araliaceae (Ginseng Family)

Indicator Value/Significance to Forest Management

Devil's club is a shade-tolerant, nitrophytic shrub that is a good indicator of nutrient rich soils with very moist to wet soil moisture regimes, usually associated with seepage areas and high precipitation. These soils develop moder and mull humus forms under boreal, cool-temperate, and cool-mesothermal climates.

Devil's club is common, and sometimes dominant, on water-receiving (floodplain, seepage, stream-bank) and water-collecting (rich wetlands) sites where it forms understory thickets in moist, par-tially open to closed, lowland forests. It occurs

	Poor	Medium	Rich
Wet			■
Moist			
Fresh			
Dry			

occasionally on water-shedding sites where there are calcareous soils. Its frequency of occur-rence increases with increasing precipitation and continentality. Associated species include red baneberry, lady fern, sweet-scented bedstraw, oak fern, sword fern, three-leaved foamflower, one-leaved foamflower (*Tiarella unifoliata* Hook.), and stream violet (*Viola glabella* Nutt.).

Although devil's club may dominate the preharvest shrub layer in a stand, typically few individuals remain after logging and the species does not pose a threat to regeneration, pro-vided planting is done immediately after cutting.

Distribution and Habitat

Distribution: Southwestern Yukon, south through western and central British Columbia, disjunct on Porphyry Island near Thunder Bay, Ont. Devil's club has been designated as a rare species in the Yukon and Ontario; in the United States, it is threatened in Michigan.

Habitat: Moist woods and clearings.

Devil's Club
Aralie épineuse

Description

General: Densely prickly, sparsely branched, straggling deciduous shrub, less than 2 m tall, with ropy stems; forming open to nearly impenetrable colonies; young stems armed with needle-sharp spines up to 1 cm long; older stems with strong spines and gray-brown papery bark.

Leaves: Alternate; very large (20–40 cm across), maple-leaf shaped, the lobes numbering 5 or more; dark green above, paler below, with spines along the prominent veins; margins sharply toothed; stalk very spiny and about as long as the blade.

Flowers: Numerous, small, greenish-white; in stalked, dense clusters along the axis of a narrow inflorescence 10–20 cm long.

Fruit: Bright red, berry-like drupe, 4–6 mm long, slightly flattened and longer than wide.

Phenology: Flowers bloom in July; the seeds ripen in August.

Synonym: *Echinopanax horridus* (Sm.) Dcne. & Planch.

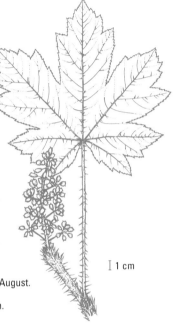

⊺ 1 cm

Notes   Devil's club berries are considered inedible, possibly because the plants are so spiny that harvesting them is difficult. The Haida rubbed the berries into the scalp to combat lice and to make the hair shiny. The spines are toxic and scratches caused by them soon become swollen and painful. This species has the ability to concentrate copper and may have value in geobotanical studies.

Oxycoccus microcarpus Turcz.
Ericaceae (Heath Family)

Indicator Value/Significance to Forest Management

Small cranberry is a shade-intolerant vine characteristic of wet, nutrient poor, organic soils. It occurs in open bogs, fens, and black spruce and larch peatlands, in close association with sphagnum mosses, under boreal, cool-temperate, and cool-mesothermal climatic regimes. These habitats are oligotrophic, with low pH levels, few exchangeable cations, and little available nitrogen and phosphorus. In British Columbia, this species increases in frequency with increasing latitude and continentality. In the southern Boreal Forest Region in Ontario, small cranberry

	Poor	Medium	Rich
Wet	■		
Moist	■		
Fresh			
Dry			

is indicative of very oligotrophic, low shrub and graminoid rich, treed bogs with poorly decomposed peat and a surface-level water table. Species with similar indicator values include round-leaved sundew (*Drosera rotundifolia* L.), bog-laurel, Labrador-tea, cloudberry, and several species of the moss genus *Sphagnum*. This diminutive plant enhances peatland biodiversity by providing food resources for pollinating insects.

Distribution and Habitat

Distribution: Yukon, Northwest Territories, British Columbia, east to Labrador and Newfoundland; absent in the high arctic, prairie regions of Alberta and Saskatchewan, and extreme southwestern Ontario.

Habitat: Wet, acidic soils in peatlands, heaths, and tundra; occasionally in moist, upland, moss-covered coniferous forests.

Small Cranberry
Airelle canneberge

Description

General: Tiny, creeping, evergreen vine; stems slender, wiry, thread-like, often rooting at the nodes, up to 50 cm long; branches erect or ascending, up to 20 cm tall; often forming small colonies on peatland hummocks or raised microfeatures of the forest floor because they spread vegetatively by runners and creeping stems.

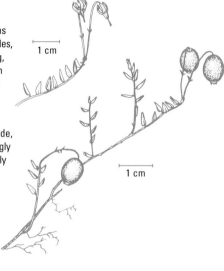

Leaves: Alternate; 2–10 mm long, 1–3 mm wide, triangular-ovate; dark, shiny green above, strongly whitened below; margins smooth, rolling strongly towards the undersurface.

Flowers: In clusters of 1–6, on stalks arising from the ends of leafy branches; stalks with 2 small bracts at or below the middle; flowers nodding; 4 pink petals, 5–6 mm long, recurved back to form a "Turk's cap", the 8 stamens forming a prominent "beak".

Fruit: Globular berry, reddish when ripe, 5–15 mm across.

Phenology: Flowers bloom in late June and July; the fruit ripens from August to October, often persisting on the plant over winter.

Synonyms: *Vaccinium oxycoccus* L.

Notes   The ripe, bitter berries of small cranberry are edible and often used to make tart preserves and juices. There is some evidence to suggest that the juice may be effective as a preventative and as a treatment for urinary tract infections.

Prunus pensylvanica L.f.
Rosaceae (Rose Family)

Indicator Value/Significance to Forest Management

Pin cherry is a shade-intolerant, fast-growing, short-lived shrub or small tree characteristic of nutrient medium, moderately coarse to coarse-textured, dry to fresh soils on water-shedding (rocky ridges, cliffs, dry woods, clearings) and water-receiving (sandy and gravelly banks, shores of rivers and lakes) sites. It is absent on wet soils. This species is infrequent to common in forest habitats, and tends to occur more often in burnt areas, clearings, disturbed areas, road-

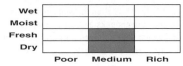

sides, fencerows, and along forest margins. In the Great Lakes–St. Lawrence Forest Region, pin cherry indicates habitats with warm, shallow, exposed soil conditions.

Pin cherry aggressively invades cleared areas and is generally more abundant in clear-cuts after burning of logging debris. This species, if not controlled, competes directly with young crop tree seedlings for moisture, nutrients, and light. Pin cherry also provides good cover for rabbits, which are capable of destroying or severely retarding the growth of planted crop trees. On the other hand, since pin cherry is so well suited to rapid colonization of large gaps in the forest, it promotes ecosystem stability by reducing soil erosion and diminishing losses of particulate organic matter and dissolved inorganic substances.

Distribution and Habitat

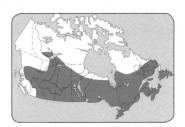

Distribution: Central British Columbia, east to Labrador and Newfoundland.

Habitat: Dry open areas, clearings, cutovers, recent burns, and forest edges.

Pin Cherry
Cerisier de Pennsylvanie

Description

General: Erect deciduous shrub or tree, mostly up to 5 m tall but reaching as much as 12 m under good growth conditions; often forming thickets; bark on young branches smooth and reddish-brown, on older branches, dark reddish-brown with conspicuous, large, orange, horizontal lenticels, bark peeling off in papery sheets.

Leaves: Alternate; commonly drooping from the twig; lanceolate, with a long taper to a slender, sharp tip, rounded at the base, 4–11 cm long; thin, hairless on both surfaces, shiny yellowish-green above, paler below; margins finely toothed with incurving teeth; stalk character-istically with a pair of large glands near the base of the leaf blade.

Flowers: In small, closely packed, roundish clusters of 5–7 flowers scattered along the branches; individual flowers about 1 cm across, with 5 white petals and numerous stamens.

Fruit: Bright red drupes, in small umbel-like clusters, 4–7 mm across, with acidic flesh and containing a large single stony seed.

Phenology: Flowers bloom with the expanding leaves, from late March through June, depending on range; the fruit matures from mid-August to September.

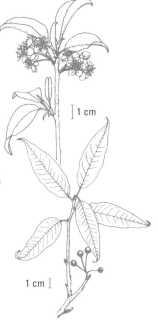

1 cm

1 cm

Notes Pin cherry is an important source of food and cover for many wildlife species. The fruit is eaten by numerous bird species. The twigs and foliage provide browse for moose, deer, and rabbits, and cover for small mammals and birds. The foliage contains hydrocyanic acid and animals browsing the leaves are known to have been poisoned. The flesh of the fruits is edible, and makes excellent jams and preserves. Aboriginal peoples added the dried fruits to pemmican for flavoring.

Rhododendron albiflorum Hook.
Ericaceae (Heath Family)

Indicator Value/Significance to Forest Management

White-flowered rhododendron is a shade-tolerant/intolerant, oxylophytic shrub that is an indicator of nutrient poor, moderately dry to fresh soils with mor humus forms in areas associated with high precipitation and late snow cover. It is common and often dominant on water-shedding sites, where it is found as high as the spruce–fir tree-line in cool, moist, open-canopy, coniferous forests. It grows in subalpine-boreal climates that are characterized by a short growing season, abundant snow, and infrequent summer moisture deficits. Its frequency of occur-

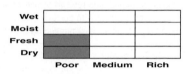

rence increases with increasing continentality and decreases with increasing latitude. Associated species include mountain huckleberry (*Vaccinium membranaceum* Dougl.), the liverwort *Barbilophozia floerkei* (Web. & Mohr) Loeske, and the moss *Rhytidiopsis robusta* (Hedw.) Broth. In southwestern Alberta, white-flowered rhododendron is one of a few shrub species, together with false azalea, mountain huckleberry, and mountain box (*Pachistima myrsinites* (Pursh) Raf.), that indicate the limits of spruce–fir stands.

Although white-flowered rhododendron has an open habit and does not produce a dense canopy, it can reduce light levels below the saturation point for Engelmann spruce (*Picea engelmannii* Parry ex Engelm.) and lodgepole pine (*Pinus contorta* Dougl. ex Loud. var. *latifolia* Engelm.) seedlings on the forest floor and maintain soil temperatures below critical thresholds for water and nutrient uptake. However, since regrowth of white-flowered rhododendron is slow following shrub removal or site scarification, prompt planting of crop species may be sufficient to prevent overtopping of seedlings. White-flowered rhododendron is a member of a complex of ericaceous shrubs that dominates mesic and drier sites in many high-elevation habitats.

Distribution and Habitat

Distribution: Southern two-thirds of British Columbia, at higher elevations.

Habitat: Coniferous forests on mountain slopes near the alpine tree-line.

White-Flowered Rhododendron
Rhododendron à fleurs blanches

Description

General: Erect, slender-branched deciduous shrub, up to 2 m tall, with exfoliating bark and young twigs covered by coarse, reddish hairs; often forming dense, impenetrable thickets.

Leaves: Alternate; narrowly elliptic to oblanceolate, acute-tipped, tapering at the base; green above, paler below, covered with loose, rusty hairs; margins smooth to wavy.

Flowers: In clusters of 1–4 flowers, borne below the new year's growth in the axils of the previous year's leaves; on glandular-hairy stalks up to 1.5 cm long; corolla whitish, bell-shaped, up to 2 cm long, with 5 broad, rounded lobes about equalling the tube in length; sepals large, oblanceolate.

Fruit: Oval-shaped capsule, 6–8 mm long, splitting to release numerous minute, winged seeds for wind-dispersal.

Phenology: Flowers bloom in mid- to late June following leaf expansion; the seeds mature in late summer.

1 cm

1 cm

Notes White-flowered rhododendron is generally unpalatable to livestock and ungulates. Serious poisoning has been reported in children after ingestion of leaves and flowers of this species.

Rhododendron canadense (L.) Torr.
Ericaceae (Heath Family)

Indicator Value/Significance to Forest Management

Rhodora is a shade-intolerant, oxylophytic shrub characteristic of acidic soil conditions with low available nitrogen levels over a range of wet to very dry soil moisture regimes. It is common in peat bogs, damp thickets, on dry heaths, acidic barrenlands, and rocky slopes. In the St. Lawrence Lowlands and Appalachian Highlands of southern Ontario, southern Quebec, and southern New Brunswick, rhodora often invades domed bogs following fire. On drier sites in Newfoundland, it is sparse in closed-canopy balsam fir or balsam fir–black spruce

	Poor	Medium	Rich
Wet	█		
Moist	█		
Fresh	█		
Dry	█		

stands, becoming abundant following clearcutting, fire, or heavy insect infestation. It is usually associated with Labrador-tea, sheep-laurel, mountain-holly, and wild-raisin (*Viburnum cassinoides* L.).

Rhodora may form moderately dense colonies which can compete with coniferous crop species on nutrient poor sites, preventing or hindering regeneration.

Distribution and Habitat

Distribution: Extreme eastern Ontario, through southern Quebec to the Maritimes and Newfoundland.

Habitat: Peaty wetlands, wet margins of ponds, damp thickets, heaths, and rocky slopes.

Rhodora
Rhododendron du Canada

Description

General: Low deciduous shrub, 60–100 cm tall, with stiffly ascending branches, leaves and showy, purple flowers.

Leaves: Alternate; elliptic to oblanceolate, blunt to acute at the tip, wedge-shaped at the base, 2–6 cm long; dark green above, paler beneath, softly hairy; margins smooth, rolling towards the undersurface.

Flowers: In few-flowered clusters **(a)** at the ends of the twigs; individual flowers showy, about 2 cm across, rose-colored to purplish, on short glandular stalks; corolla 2–3 cm long, split nearly to the short, tubular base into 3 parts, the 2 lower parts oblong and spreading, the upper one shallowly 3-lobed.

Fruit: Dry, 5-part, many-seeded capsule **(b)** with a purplish bloom, softly hairy, 1–1.5 cm long; empty capsules remain on the twigs through the winter.

Phenology: Flowers bloom in May and June, just before or with the expanding leaves; the seeds mature in July and August, dispersed during the fall.

a

b

1 cm

Notes Rhodora has been reported to cause serious poisoning in children after ingestion of the leaves and flowers.

Ribes lacustre (Pers.) Poir.
Saxifragaceae (Saxifrage Family)

Indicator Value/Significance to Forest Management

Bristly black currant is a shade-tolerant/intolerant, nitrophytic shrub that is a good indicator of nutrient rich, fine-textured, neutral to slightly basic soils with fresh to moist soil moisture regimes. These soils typically develop moder and mull humus forms in boreal, temperate, and cool-mesothermal climates. This species occurs most frequently on water-receiving sites in semi-open forests and less often on water-shedding sites in similar habitats. Associated species with similar indicator values include Rocky Mountain maple (*Acer glabrum* Torr.), red baneberry, wild sarsaparilla, dwarf raspberry, star-flowered false Solomon's-seal (*Smilacina stellata* (L.) Desf.), and Sitka valerian (*Valeriana sitchensis* Bong.). In the northern hardwoods of Quebec, bristly black currant occurs within yellow birch–black ash stands in small catchment basins with water-logged soils. On these sites, it is often associated with wild-raisin (*Viburnum cassinoides* L.), speckled alder, and various species of the moss genus *Sphagnum*.

	Poor	Medium	Rich
Wet			
Moist			██
Fresh			██
Dry			

In British Columbia, bristly black currant is a common member of a shrub association that poses serious competition problems for crop tree regeneration on rich, productive, alluvial sites. By itself, however, the species does not reach cover levels that are seriously detrimental to conifer seedlings. In the Boreal Forest Region of northern Ontario, bristly black currant competes for light in the early stages of conifer stand establishment. This species is also an alternate host of white pine blister rust (*Cronartium ribicola* J.C. Fischer).

Distribution and Habitat

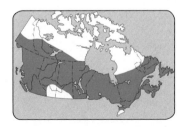

Distribution: Yukon and British Columbia, east to Labrador and Newfoundland.

Habitat: In thickets, moist woods, and swamps, on slopes, along lakeshores, and in riparian habitats; prefers calcareous, fine-textured soils.

Bristly Black Currant
Gadellier lacustre

Description

General: Low, erect or straggling deciduous shrub, generally less than 1 m tall, arising from a poorly developed rhizome; young branches densely covered with prickles, longer spines at the nodes; older branches with grayish, peeling bark and fewer prickles; growing singly or in extensive low thickets.

Leaves: Alternate; blade palmately divided into 3–5 lobes, base heart-shaped, 2.5–6 cm wide; margins coarsely toothed.

Flowers: In slender, drooping, elongate clusters, about 2.5 cm long; individual flowers yellowish-green, saucer-shaped, less than 6 mm across; stalk and calyx densely covered with gland-tipped hairs.

Fruit: Bristly, dark purple or black berry, 5–12 mm across; dispersed both by gravity and by birds and mammals.

Phenology: Flowers bloom in May and June; the seeds ripen from late July to August.

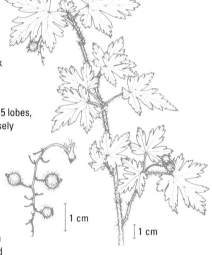

1 cm

1 cm

Notes The berries are utilized for food by some wildlife, in particular squirrels, skunks, and many species of birds, but are of minor importance to ungulates. The berries are edible but are disagreeable to the taste. The spines may produce a serious allergic reaction in some people.

Rubus chamaemorus L.
Rosaceae (Rose Family)

Indicator Value/Significance to Forest Management

Cloudberry is a shade-tolerant/intolerant, oxylophytic dwarf shrub that is an excellent indicator of nutrient poor, moist to wet, mineral or organic soils. Across the Boreal Forest Region, it is characteristically found in black spruce peatlands. In Newfoundland, it is often present in wet black spruce stands with a ground cover dominated by sedges and sphagnum mosses. In the wetlands of Atlantic Canada, it is associated with bog communities in habitats ranging from relatively dry sites in the Maritimes and central Newfoundland to wet bog hollows and

	Poor	Medium	Rich
Wet	▓		
Moist	▓		
Fresh			
Dry			

flats in northern Newfoundland and Labrador. Commonly associated species include three-leaved false Solomon's-seal (*Smilacina trifolia* (L.) Desf.), three-fruited sedge (*Carex trisperma* Dew.), common green sphagnum, black crowberry (*Empetrum nigrum* L.), and low sweet blue-berry (*Vaccinium angustifolium* Ait.).

Distribution and Habitat

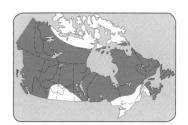

Distribution: Yukon, British Columbia, east through northern Alberta and Saskatchewan, Manitoba, north-ern Ontario and Quebec, to the Maritimes, Labrador and Newfoundland. Cloudberry has been designated as a rare species in Prince Edward Island.

Habitat: In sphagnum mats and on moist to wet mineral soils, in black spruce bogs and on mossy tundra.

Cloudberry • Bakeapple
Chicouté

Description

General: Low deciduous shrub, arising from a slender, creeping, woody rhizome, with upright, unbranched and unarmed flowering stems, 10–30 cm high; bearing leaves only at the upper 1–3 stem nodes, lower nodes with small stipules only.

Leaves: Alternate; on long stalks, 2–8 cm long; round, with 5–7 rounded lobes separated by rather shallow notches; dark green, rough-textured; margins finely toothed with blunt teeth; stipules sheathing the stem.

Flowers: Solitary on a long terminal stalk; showy, 2–3 cm across, with 5 spreading, white petals; male **(a)** and female flowers on separate plants.

Fruit: Raspberry-like, composed of a few, large-seeded drupelets **(b)**; reddish at first, then turning yellow at maturity; falling quickly from the dry receptacle.

Phenology: Flowers bloom in June and July; the fruit matures in late August and September.

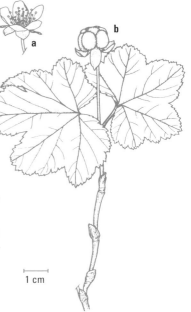

a

b

1 cm

Notes   Cloudberry fruit is edible, with a distinctive baked-apple flavor that sometimes requires getting used to. They can be eaten with sugar and cream, cooked and made into an excellent jam, or distilled and made into a liqueur.

Rubus parviflorus Nutt.
Rosaceae (Rose Family)

Indicator Value/Significance to Forest Management

Thimbleberry is a shade-tolerant/intolerant, nitrophytic shrub that is an indicator of nutrient rich soils with moder and mull humus forms. It is common on water-receiving sites in open-canopy forests and early-seral communities, and is most abundant on fresh, well-aerated soils in seepage habitats. Thimbleberry may be found on drier or wetter soils, but growth on these sites is stunted and cover values typically remain low. Its frequency of occurrence in British Columbia decreases with increasing elevation and latitude, and increases with increasing

continentality. Associated species include red alder (*Alnus rubra* Bong.), lady fern, fireweed, devil's club, salmonberry, red-berry elder (*Sambucus callicarpa* Greene), rose twisted stalk (*Streptopus roseus* Michx.), and one-leaved foamflower (*Tiarella unifoliata* Hook.).

Thimbleberry is an important competitor of conifers, particularly in central British Columbia where it very rapidly and aggressively takes over clearcut areas. In this region, its dense canopy of large leaves causes greater and more rapid mortality of young conifer seedlings than any other shrub species. Thimbleberry that is present before logging resprouts from rhizomes and may rapidly increase in cover and vigor following canopy removal. This species can also quickly colonize cleared sites through germination of buried seeds. Thimbleberry cover declines as a tree canopy is formed.

Distribution and Habitat

Distribution: Southern and central British Columbia, Alberta, Cypress Hills in Saskatchewan, isolated populations in the upper Great Lakes basin.

Habitat: Mostly in open habitats, including open forests, along forest margins and lakeshores, and on talus slopes.

Thimbleberry
Ronce parviflore

Description

General: Erect, much-branched deciduous shrub, 1–2.5 m tall, arising from a vigorous rhizome; often forming dense thickets; stems unarmed, green to brownish, glandular-hairy; older stems purplish-red to gray-brown, with exfoliating papery bark; when open-grown, producing a dense, multilayered canopy and very large leaf areas.

Leaves: Alternate; large (10–20 cm across), maple-leaf shaped, usually with 3–5 triangular lobes; margins irregularly sharp-toothed; lower surface soft-hairy.

‖ 1 cm

Flowers: In terminal clusters of 3–10 flowers; individual flowers white, showy, 3–5 cm across, 5 petals, 5 sepals with long tail-like tips.

Fruit: Raspberry-like, pink to red, composed of large juicy drupelets, very soft when ripe.

Phenology: Flowers bloom in June and July; the fruit ripens and falls to the ground in late July and August; wider dispersal is by birds and mammals that feed on the fruit.

Notes   The foliage and twigs of thimbleberry are of low to moderate importance as a food source for wildlife, but the fruit is consumed by many species of birds and mammals. The fruit is edible but lacks flavor, and has a coarse, seedy texture. Young sprouts of the plant were used as a green vegetable by aboriginal peoples in British Columbia.

Rubus pubescens Raf.
Rosaceae (Rose Family)

Indicator Value/Significance to Forest Management

Dwarf raspberry is a shade-tolerant/intolerant, nitrophytic species that is an indicator of nutrient rich, fresh, moist, or wet soils. These rich soils typically develop moder and mull humus forms in boreal, continental, and temperate climates. Dwarf raspberry is a scattered understory species in thickets and deciduous, coniferous, and mixed forests on water-receiving sites.
In the Boreal Forest Region, dwarf raspberry is most often associated with balsam poplar and trembling aspen stands, but also occurs in coniferous forests. It shows moderate regional presence values for

	Poor	Medium	Rich
Wet			
Moist			
Fresh			
Dry			

white spruce–balsam fir stands between Great Slave Lake and the Cape Breton Highlands in Nova Scotia, and for black spruce stands between north-central British Columbia and northeast-ern Ontario, and in Newfoundland. In west-central Alberta, dwarf raspberry has a tendency to have higher cover on more productive sites. In wetland habitats in the southern sections of the Boreal Forest Region in Ontario, this species is associated with hardwood swamps on alluvial sites having neutral to slightly basic, nutrient rich, silt and clay-textured soils. In the northern hardwoods of Quebec, dwarf raspberry occurs within sugar maple and yellow birch–black ash stands in small catchment basins with water-logged soils. In this region, it is often associated on wet sites with sensitive fern, cinnamon fern (*Osmunda cinnamomea* L.), and various species of the moss genus *Sphagnum*, and on moist to fresh sites with lady fern and wild-raisin (*Viburnum cassinoides* L.).

Distribution and Habitat

Distribution: Yukon and British Columbia, east to Labrador and Newfoundland. Dwarf raspberry has been designated as a rare species in the Yukon; in the United States, it is rare in Colorado, Iowa, and Wyoming.

Habitat: Deciduous, coniferous, and mixed forests, thickets, clearings, peaty wetlands, along streams.

Dwarf Raspberry • Dewberry
Ronce pubescente

Description

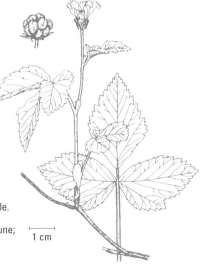

General: Trailing, unarmed, deciduous perennial, with runner-like stems and erect, herbaceous, leafy branches, 10–30 cm tall.

Leaves: Alternate; compound; composed of 3 leaflets, each 2–7 cm long, terminal leaflet diamond-shaped, with a sharp tip; margins sharply toothed; stipules prominent, oval-shaped, and sharp-pointed.

Flowers: Solitary or in loose terminal clusters, on slender, glandular-hairy stalks; individual flowers with 5, white to pale pink, erect petals.

Fruit: Raspberry-like, bright red, composed of large juicy drupelets, difficult to separate from the receptacle.

Phenology: Flowers bloom in late May and early June; the fruit ripens from July to September.

1 cm

Notes   The fruit is edible but is smaller and less tasty than those of wild red raspberry (*R. idaeus* L.).

Rubus spectabilis Pursh
Rosaceae (Rose Family)

Indicator Value/Significance to Forest Management

Salmonberry is a shade-tolerant, nitrophytic shrub that is a good indicator of nutrient rich, very moist to wet soils with moder and mull humus forms. It favors a humid to perhumid coastal climate with relatively mild temperatures and a lengthy growing season. Salmonberry occurs on water-receiving sites in lowland forests, on moist slopes, and on streambanks, with best growth occurring on floodplain soils that are well-aerated and near field water capacity. It is found on a range of soil textures from rich loams to loamy clays. Its frequency of occurrence increases

	Poor	Medium	Rich
Wet			██
Moist			██
Fresh			
Dry			

with increasing precipitation, and decreases with increasing elevation and continentality. At higher elevations, this species becomes restricted to streambank habitats. Associated species include red alder (*Alnus rubra* Bong.), lady fern, western skunk cabbage, devil's club, thimbleberry, and three-leaved foamflower.

Salmonberry often develops into dense thickets after logging. On sites where it is present in the understory before logging, canopy removal results in a rapid increase in colony size, crown cover, and stand diversity. Salmonberry is a major competitor of young conifers on moist, productive sites throughout most of coastal British Columbia. Dense thickets of salmonberry inhibit establishment of natural and planted conifers by reducing light penetration to the forest floor. On the other hand, these dense colonies can also act to reduce soil erosion and inhibit invasion of long-lived deciduous species such as red alder, bigleaf maple (*Acer macrophyllum* Pursh), and black cottonwood (*Populus trichocarpa* Torr. & A. Gray).

Distribution and Habitat

Distribution: Coastal British Columbia.

Habitat: Moist forests and swampy places at low to medium elevations.

Salmonberry
Ronce remarquable

Description

General: Erect, biennial, deciduous shrub, 0.6–3 m tall; stems strongly bristly, especially below, arising from a branching rhizome; forming extensive, nearly impenetrable thickets.

Leaves: Alternate, on long stalks; compound, composed of 3 diamond-shaped to oval leaflets; margins sharply toothed.

Flowers: Solitary on short leafy twigs; large and showy, about 3 cm across, with deep pink, triangular petals.

Fruit: Ovoid, raspberry-like, red or yellow when ripe; dispersed mainly by birds and mammals.

Phenology: Flowers bloom between April and June in the south, and from April to July in the north; the fruit reaches maturity between early June or July in southern low-lying areas, and in August in northern areas or at higher elevations.

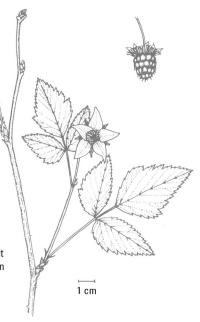

1 cm

Notes   Both the sprouts and berries of salmonberry were eaten in large quantities by all coastal aboriginal peoples in British Columbia.

Shepherdia canadensis (L.) Nutt.
Elaeagnaceae (Oleaster Family)

Indicator Value/Significance to Forest Management

Soapberry is a shade-intolerant shrub characteristic of very dry to moderately dry, light sandy soils with low to medium nutrient levels. This species is symbiotic with nitrogen-fixing organisms. It occurs in a variety of habitats in open to semi-open, coniferous and mixed forests on water-shedding sites (uplands, shallow soils on rock outcrops, or well-drained, coarse-skeletal soils). In British Columbia, its frequency of occurrence increases with increasing continentality. Soapberry is often a dominant shrub in the understory of pine and pine–spruce forests

	Poor	Medium	Rich
Wet			
Moist			
Fresh			
Dry			

in British Columbia and Alberta. It is found in pine stands throughout the Boreal Forest Region. In spruce-dominated forests, soapberry shows high regional presence values in white spruce-balsam fir stands from Alaska to central Alberta, but is infrequent in black spruce stands. Associated species include purple reedgrass (*Calamagrostis rubescens* Buckley), twinflower (*Linnaea borealis* L.), mountain box (*Pachistima myrsinites* [Pursh] Raf.), mountain cranberry, and bearberry.

Distribution and Habitat

Distribution: Yukon, Northwest Territories, British Columbia, east to Newfoundland, scattered occurrences in northern Quebec and Labrador.

Habitat: Sandy, gravelly, or rocky soils; in open woods, along lakeshores and streams, on dry slopes.

Soapberry • Buffaloberry
Shépherdie du Canada

Description

General: Low to medium-sized, much-branched deciduous shrub, up to 2 m tall, with rust-colored, scurfy stems; older stems are grayish-brown and smooth.

Leaves: Opposite; elliptic or oval, with a rounded tip and a rounded or tapered base, 1.5–5 cm long; dull, dark-green and occasionally hairy above, silvery and scurfy, with rusty scales below; margins smooth; stalk about 1 cm long, grooved and rust-colored, scurfy.

Flowers: Male and female flowers mostly occurring on separate plants; clustered in the leaf axils of the previous year's growth; individual flowers very small, unisexual, 3–4 mm across, yellowish, with 4 petals.

Fruit: Bright red, berry-like drupe, covered with rust-colored scales, about 5 mm across, containing 3–5 nutlets.

Phenology: Flowers bloom from late April to mid-June, depending on the region, before the leaves emerge; the seeds ripen in late June or July.

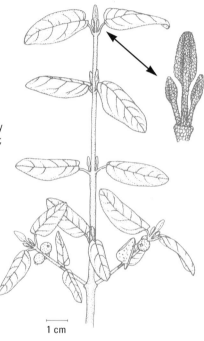

1 cm

Notes The fruit has a bitter, nauseating taste when eaten raw, but becomes a tasty treat when mixed with sugar and water and beaten into a frothy mass (hence the common name soapberry). The fruit is an important food source for birds. This shrub has the ability to bioaccumulate mercury and zinc, which may be useful for the detection of soil contamination.

Trees and Shrubs

Spiraea douglasii Hook.
Rosaceae (Rose Family)

Indicator Value/Significance to Forest Management

Western hardhack is a shade-intolerant shrub that is an indicator of moist to wet, nutrient poor to nutrient medium soils with moderate levels of soil nitrogen. It prefers saturated mor and moder humus forms, typically underlain by organic or gleyed mineral soils, that are developed under cool-mesothermal climates.

This species often indicates sites with cold air drainage (frost pockets). It is characteristic of disturbed, water-receiving and water-collecting sites in the Coast Forest Region, where it is common to occasionally dominant in semi-terrestrial communities (wetlands) and open-canopy forests. Western hardhack tolerates fluctuating water tables. Its frequency of occurrence decreases with increasing latitude, elevation, and continentality. Western hardhack often occurs in association with salal.

	Poor	Medium	Rich
Wet	███	███	
Moist	███	███	
Fresh			
Dry			

Western hardhack will invade and grow vigorously on productive forest sites and is capable of inhibiting the establishment and growth of crop tree species.

Distribution and Habitat

Distribution: Coastal and southern British Columbia. Two subspecies occur: subspecies *douglasii* has densely hairy lower leaf surfaces, and is confined to coastal areas; subspecies *menziesii* (Hook.) Presl has lower leaf surfaces that are less hairy; it is more widespread, occurring from the coast, east to the Columbia River valley in southeastern British Columbia.

Habitat: Wetlands and moist meadows at low to subalpine elevations.

Western Hardhack
Spirée de Douglas

Description

General: Low deciduous shrub, up to 2 m tall; with erect, densely hairy stems, alternate leaves, and numerous small flowers in terminal clusters.

Leaves: Alternate; elliptic to oblong, with a rounded tip and a rounded to tapering base; margins coarsely toothed towards the tip; lower surface densely hairy.

Flowers: In dense, elongate clusters arising from the upper leaf axils and the end of the stem; individual flowers with 5, pink to rose-colored petals.

Fruit: Shiny follicles, 2.5–3 mm long, hairless except along the sutures, containing many small seeds.

Phenology: Flowers bloom in May and June.

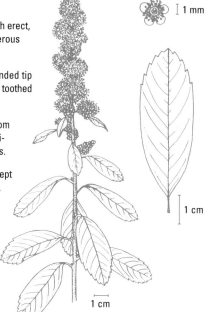

1 mm

1 cm

1 cm

Notes   The twigs of western hardhack were used by aboriginal peoples as blades, scrapers, and roasting sticks, as hooks to dry and smoke salmon, and as tools for harvesting dentalium shells.

Taxus canadensis Marsh.
Taxaceae (Yew Family)

Indicator Value/Significance to Forest Management

American yew is a shade-tolerant/intolerant shrub that is a moderate indicator of fresh to moist, mineral and organic soils, particularly soils associated with seepage zones. It is commonly associated with semi-closed to closed-canopy forests, especially deciduous and eastern white cedar stands. Within the Great Lakes–St. Lawrence Forest Region, this species is characteristic of moist, moderately fertile soils with thick, raw, acidic humus supporting stands dominated by hemlock and other conifers. However, at least in the mixed white spruce–balsam fir–yellow

birch forests of Quebec, this species is considered to be a poor indicator of site conditions. In mixed forests dominated by sugar maple and coniferous species on shallow, loamy soils over limestone bedrock, American yew sometimes forms dense, impenetrable colonies growing to over 2 m high. In boreal Newfoundland, American yew is commonly associated with balsam fir on middle to lower slopes in limestone rich habitats. Associated species include goldthread, stairstep moss, mayflower, and rose twisted stalk (*Streptopus roseus* Michx.).

Distribution and Habitat

Distribution: Southeast Manitoba, east through central and southern Ontario and Quebec, the Maritimes, and Newfoundland; reports from Labrador require confirmation.

Habitat: Thickets and coniferous, deciduous and mixed forests, on ravine slopes and rocky banks.

American Yew • Canada Yew • Ground-Hemlock
If du Canada

Description

General: Low, spreading, evergreen shrub, generally less than 2 m tall; with branches spreading out from the base of the plant for about one-third of their length before curving upwards; often forming dense colonies.

Leaves: Flat linear needles; 1–2.5 cm long, 1–3 mm wide; short-stalked; tip abruptly narrowed to a short sharp point; dark green and shiny above, paler below; spirally arranged on the branches but the stalks are twisted so that the leaves form 2 flat rows along each branch.

Reproductive Structures: Small, cone-like, inconspicuous, borne singly in the leaf axils; male and female parts usually on separate plants; male cones consisting of stalked clusters of pollen sacs extending from a basal cluster of small bracts; female structure erect and green, consisting of a single, minute ovary on a short stalk and subtended by several small scales.

1 cm

a

Seed-Bearing Structure: A cup-like, bright red, pulpy aril **(a)**, 5–10 mm across, open at the free end, surrounding a single, green to brown, stony seed.

Phenology: Pollination occurs in early spring; the seeds ripen in August.

Notes The foliage of American yew is heavily browsed by deer and moose. The red, fleshy aril is sweet-tasting and edible, but the seed and the rest of the plant, particularly wilted foliage, are reported to be toxic to humans and some animals. The seed may pass safely through the digestive tract if not chewed. The foliage is reported to have been used in the making of a beverage by several aboriginal groups in Quebec and the Michigan region of the United States.

Vaccinium parvifolium Sm.
Ericaceae (Heath Family)

Indicator Value/Significance to Forest Management

Red huckleberry is a shade-tolerant shrub that is a good indicator of nitrogen poor soils. It grows under a cool-mesothermal climatic regime and occurs in coastal, coniferous forests on raw humus and decaying wood. Its frequency of occurrence decreases with increasing elevation and continentality.

Distribution and Habitat

Distribution: Coastal British Columbia, inland to the Columbia River, but rare away from the coast.

Habitat: Raw humus and decaying wood in coniferous forests, especially along the edges of clearings and along trails; from sea level to 400 m above sea level near the coast, to 1000 m above sea level in the interior.

Red Huckleberry • Red Bilberry
Airelle à petites feuilles

Description

1 mm

General: Erect, crown-forming deciduous shrub, usually 1–2.5 m tall but may reach 7 m; with slender, green, prominently angled young branches.

Leaves: Alternate; oval to oblong-elliptic, obtuse-tipped, 1–2.5 cm long, 8–14 mm wide; smooth above, short-hairy below; margins smooth.

Flowers: Solitary, on short stalks from the leaf axils; corolla globular to urn-shaped, 4–6 mm long, waxy, pink to yellowish-green.

Fruit: Bright red berry, 7–9 mm across.

Phenology: Flowers bloom from April to June.

1 cm

Notes   The berries are edible and have a good, but sour, flavor. They make a tasty jelly.

Vaccinium vitis-idaea L. var. *minus* Lodd.
Ericaceae (Heath Family)

Indicator Value/Significance to Forest Management

Mountain cranberry is a shade-intolerant, oxylophytic shrub that is an indicator of nutrient poor, coarse-textured soils over a wide range of soil moisture regimes. In the southern part of its range, it occurs most frequently in wetlands and on relatively moist sites; farther north it frequents dry to moist soils or those that are well to moderately drained. Best growth is achieved on soils that retain some moisture throughout the growing season. Mountain cranberry is strongly associated with open bogs and jack pine stands throughout the Boreal Forest

	Poor	Medium	Rich
Wet			
Moist			
Fresh			
Dry			

Region. It shows a high regional presence value for white spruce–balsam fir stands west of Manitoba, but is absent or infrequent in these stands in the east. In black spruce stands, mountain cranberry shows a bimodal regional distribution pattern, with high presence values in stands west of Saskatchewan and in Newfoundland. Although its seeds can germinate on bare ground, if conditions are favorable, mountain cranberry is not a pioneer species. It often forms a seral community with black crowberry (*Empetrum nigrum L.)* and other mat-forming woody species. Mountain cranberry is successionally displaced over time by black spruce and balsam fir. Low light intensities limit its growth and reproduction and thus canopy closure eventually brings about its elimination from these stands. Mountain cranberry may be found, however, in successionally advanced jack pine stands having thin humus layers.

Distribution and Habitat

Distribution: Widespread in north temperate, boreal, and arctic regions; in Canada, its range extends from the Yukon and British Columbia to Newfoundland.

Habitat: Occupies a wide range of habitats; in extreme exposures on headlands, sea cliffs, rocky hilltops, eskers, and mountain summits, in black and white spruce, jack pine, and mixed forests, and in open wetlands, especially bogs.

Mountain Cranberry • Partridgeberry • Lingonberry
Airelle vigne-d'Ida

Description

General: Creeping, dwarf evergreen shrub; stems semi-woody, hairy, bark with a reddish tinge in late autumn; branches up to 15 cm high; occasionally producing rhizomes which are similar in appearance to the stems.

Leaves: Alternate; numerous, crowded on the stem; oval, but broadest towards the tip, 5–18 mm long, 3–9 mm wide; somewhat leathery, upper surface (a) dark green and shiny, turning bright red in autumn, lower surface (b) waxy, pale green, with black glandular dots; margins smooth, rolling towards the undersurface.

Flowers: Singly or in terminal clusters of 3–6 nodding, pink or reddish flowers; corolla bell-shaped, about 6 mm long, with 4 slightly reflexed lobes; the plants do not generally flower until 14–20 years of age.

Fruit: Shiny, bright red, globular berry, 6–10 mm across; berries may remain on the plant throughout the winter and into the following spring; seeds are dispersed in the droppings of birds and mammals.

Phenology: Flowers bloom from mid-June to early August; the berries mature in late August or early September.

Notes   Mountain cranberries are used as a food source by many species of wildlife, especially grouse, songbirds, black bears, and chipmunks. The sour, bitter berries have a characteristic tart flavor that improves after the first frost; they are used for the preparation of pies, preserves, and other foods.

Herbs
and
Grasses

Achlys triphylla (Sm.) DC.
Berberidaceae (Barberry Family)

Indicator Value/Significance to Forest Management

Vanilla leaf is a shade-tolerant/intolerant, nitrophytic herb that is a good indicator of nutrient rich, moist seepage soils, particularly soils rich in nitrogen and developing moder and mull humus forms. However, it will tolerate drier sites if growing on base-rich parent materials. This species is often found under a dense canopy of Douglas-fir and western hemlock in submontane to montane habitats where the climatic regime ranges from maritime to submaritime with cool-mesothermal characteristics. The occurrence of vanilla leaf decreases with increasing

	Poor	Medium	Rich
Wet			
Moist			▓
Fresh			
Dry			

latitude, elevation, and continentality. On Vancouver Island, a ground cover of vanilla leaf and sword fern indicates high site quality for the growth of Douglas-fir (*Pseudotsuga menziesii* (Mirb. Franco). Vanilla leaf and sword fern are often associated.

Distribution and Habitat

Distribution: Coastal British Columbia, from the eastern slopes of the Cascade mountain range to the coast; more plentiful on Vancouver Island than on the mainland.

Habitat: Usually in deep woods but also in more open areas, especially along streams. Two chromosomal races occur in British Columbia: diploids and tetraploids; diploids are found in high altitude regions, usually on slopes in full light regimes; tetraploids are found in flat, lowland regions, often in deep shade.

Vanilla Leaf • Deerfoot
Achlyde à trois folioles

Description

General: Stemless perennial herb with long-stalked trifoliate compound leaves arising from a rhizome.

Leaves: Basal; leaves 5–20 cm across, divided into 3 coarsely toothed leaflets; on a stalk 10–30 cm long.

Flowers: Numerous, in a terminal, bractless spike 2.5–5 cm long, on a 20–40 cm leafless stalk; individual flowers inconspicuous, lacking calyx and corolla.

Fruit: Reddish-purple; 3–4 mm long; slightly fleshy but becoming dry when ripe; strongly curved inner side with a prominent ridge, outer side with a slight ridge; containing 1 seed.

Phenology: Flowers bloom from April to July.

1 cm

Notes   Bundles of the leaves, hung to dry, perfume a room with a delicate vanilla scent. This species makes an attractive ornamental in west coast gardens.

Actaea rubra (Ait.) Willd.
Ranunculaceae (Buttercup Family)

Indicator Value/Significance to Forest Management

Red baneberry is a shade-tolerant, nitrophytic herb that is an indicator of seepage habitats with basic, nutrient rich soils, fresh to very fresh soil moisture regimes, and moder and mull humus forms. It occurs on water-receiving (alluvial, floodplain, seepage, and streambank) sites in regions with boreal, cool-temperate, or cool-mesothermal climates. In British Columbia, its frequency of occurrence increases with increasing precipitation and continentality. In the Boreal Forest Region, red baneberry shows high regional presence values for white spruce-

	Poor	Medium	Rich
Wet			
Moist			
Fresh			▓
Dry			

balsam fir stands between northern Alberta and central Quebec, and for black spruce stands between central Saskatchewan and northern Ontario. It is often associated with white baneberry (*Actaea pachypoda* Ell.), wild sarsaparilla, lady fern, beaked hazel, rough-fruited fairybells (*Disporum trachycarpum* [Wats.] Benth. & Hook.), sweet-scented bedstraw, shining clubmoss, wild lily-of-the-valley (*Maianthemum canadense* Desf.), bristly black currant, and squashberry (*Viburnum edule* [Michx.] Raf.) in hardwood and mixedwood stands.

Distribution and Habitat

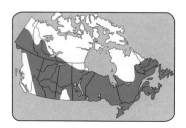

Distribution: Wide-ranging boreal forest species, from Alaska to Newfoundland.

Habitat: Rich, well-drained, moist deciduous and coniferous woodlands on floodplains, seepage areas, and stream margins.

Red Baneberry
Actée rouge

Description

General: Perennial herb, 40–80 cm tall, arising from a thick, fleshy rhizome; bearing large, widespreading compound leaves and small white flowers in a long-stalked terminal cluster.

Leaves: Alternate; large, compound, 2–3 on a stem; each leaf divided into 3 ovate leaflets, lobed or sharply toothed, hairy underneath.

Flowers: Small, white, borne in a terminal cluster; petals and petal-like sepals soon falling away; stamens numerous; single pistil with 2-lobed stigma.

Fruit: Berries bright red (rarely white), 6–13 mm long, on slender stalks that do not become thickened; terminal cluster of fruits is very conspicuous; berries are poisonous.

Phenology: Flowers bloom from April to early July; the fruit matures from August to October.

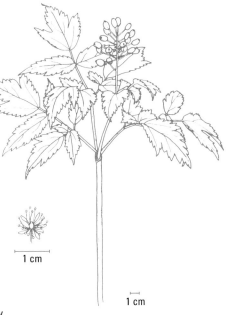

1 cm

1 cm

Notes   The berries and roots of red baneberry are **poisonous** and, if eaten, can result in vomiting, bloody diarrhea, and possibly respiratory paralysis.

Aralia nudicaulis L.
Araliaceae (Ginseng Family)

Indicator Value/Significance to Forest Management

Wild sarsaparilla is a shade-tolerant/intolerant, nitrophytic herb that is an indicator of nutrient medium to rich, fresh to moist soils which develop moder and mull humus forms under continental, boreal, and cool-temperate climates. It is found on water-shedding and water-receiving sites where it is scattered to plentiful in continental upland deciduous, coniferous, and mixedwood forests. Wild sarsaparilla is found in most boreal white spruce–balsam fir stands east of Great Slave Lake, and shows moderate regional presence value for boreal black spruce stands

between Saskatchewan and Quebec; it also occurs sporadically in black spruce stands in other areas of the Boreal Forest Region. In wetland habitats in the southern part of the Boreal Forest Region in Ontario, wild sarsaparilla is associated with seepage areas in cedar swamps having well-decomposed peaty soils. In the Great Lakes–St. Lawrence Forest Region it is indicative of acidic soils with fresh to moist soil moisture regimes and slightly infertile to fertile soil nutrient conditions. It is least abundant in deeply shaded, sugar maple ecosystems on fertile moist soils, and on wet organic soils. Flowering is more prevalent in relatively open stands. It is often associated with other rich site species such as red baneberry, large-leaved aster (*Aster macrophyllus* L.), bush honeysuckle (*Diervilla lonicera* Mill.), Hooker's fairybells (*Disporum hookeri* (Torr.) Nicholson), oak fern, false spikenard, star-flowered false Solomon's-seal (*Smilacina stellata* (L.) Desf.), and stream violet (*Viola glabella* Nutt.).

Distribution and Habitat

Distribution: Southeastern Yukon, southern District of Mackenzie, N.W.T., and eastern British Columbia, east to Labrador and Newfoundland. Wild sarsaparilla is designated as a rare species in the Yukon and continental Northwest Territories; in the United States, it is endangered in Georgia and rare in Colorado, Iowa and Missouri.

Habitat: Fresh to very moist, nitrogen rich soils in woodlands and old forests; more common in hardwoods and mixedwoods, less common in coniferous forests.

Wild Sarsaparilla
Aralie à tige nue

Description

General: Perennial herb arising from a woody rhizome; stem short, close to the ground, bearing a single, long-stalked, compound leaf 20–50 cm high, and a shorter, separate flowering stalk with 3 spherical clusters of flowers.

Leaves: Single, compound, basal leaf divided into 3 parts, each part with 3–5 leaflets; leaflets oval, pointed at the tips, 5–15 cm long, margin finely toothed; dark green above, pale green below; lowermost leaflets closest to the stem are about twice as large as the opposite leaflets.

Flowers: Small, numerous, greenish; in 2–7 spherical clusters 2–5 cm across, on top of a slender leafless flowering stalk.

Fruit: Globular berry, about 6 mm across, purplish-black; not edible.

Phenology: Flowers bloom in May and June; the fruit ripens in July and August.

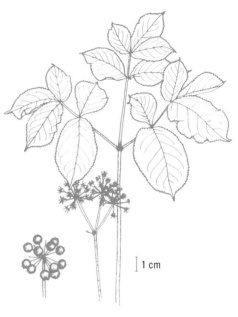

1 cm

Notes   Aboriginal peoples in British Columbia have used the rhizomes to make a refreshing drink for the relief of stomach pains. European settlers occasionally made wine from the berries, and root beer from the rhizomes. In the 1800s, sarsaparilla was highly fashionable as a spring tonic.

Asarum canadense L.
Aristolochiaceae (Birthwort Family)

Indicator Value/Significance to Forest Management

Wild ginger is a shade-tolerant, nitrophytic herb that is a good indicator of nutrient rich, fresh to moist soils with mull humus forms. It is locally common on water-receiving sites in mainly deciduous forest habitats. Seral associations range from young, successional trembling aspen–white birch stands with a beaked hazel understory in northwestern Ontario, to mature, climax hardwood forest in eastern North America. Within the northern hardwood forests of Quebec, in the Great Lakes–St. Lawrence Forest Region, wild ginger is a eutrophic herb indicative of mesic,

	Poor	Medium	Rich
Wet			
Moist			▓
Fresh			▓
Dry			

sugar maple–basswood stands that occur below 210 m elevation and are associated with limestone outcrops. In these hardwood stands, wild ginger is usually found with such species as large-flowered bellwort (*Uvularia grandiflora* Sm.), blue cohosh (*Caulophyllum thalictroides* [L.] Michx.), and trout lily. Species with similar indicator values include wild sarsaparilla, sweet-scented bedstraw, oak fern, three-leaved foamflower, and nodding trillium.

Distribution and Habitat

Distribution: Eastern North America, from south-eastern Manitoba through Ontario, Quebec to New Brunswick and southward throughout northeastern United States; in Ontario and Quebec, primarily found in the mixedwoods of the Great Lakes–St. Lawrence Forest Region.

Habitat: Relatively common in moist, rich woods, such as along riverbanks and on shaded calcareous ledges; can be found under cover of sugar maple, black ash, white cedar, bur oak, basswood, and silver maple.

Wild Ginger
Asaret du Canada

Description

General: Stemless perennial herb arising from a creeping rhizome that runs just below the soil surface; rhizome with distinctive ginger flavor; often forming colonies.

Leaves: Two basal kidney-shaped leaves, with long stalks arising directly from the rhizome; 6–18 cm across; prominently veined; dark green above, lighter below; finely hairy; leaves persist through the summer.

Flowers: Single; lying close to the ground between the 2 leaves **(a)**; reddish-brown to purplish inside; 2–4 cm long, with 3 pointed, spreading to reflexed, calyx lobes; the flowers are pollinated by crawling insects.

Fruit: Fleshy, globular capsule that breaks open releasing large, wrinkled, egg-shaped seeds.

Phenology: Flowers in April and May.

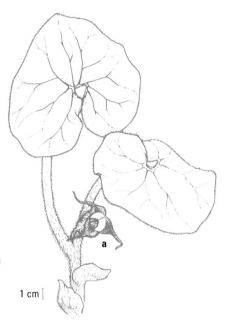

1 cm

Notes   Wild ginger, although not related to the plant from which commercial ginger is obtained, has a similar but stronger aroma and taste. The ginger-flavored rhizomes can be used fresh, or dried and powdered as a spice. The plant is reputed to have medicinal value, particularly for treating flatulence. A few cases of dermatitis from handling the leaves have been reported.

Calamagrostis canadensis (Michx.) Beauv.
Poaceae (Grass Family)

Indicator Value/Significance to Forest Management

Bluejoint grass is a shade-tolerant/intolerant grass that is a good indicator of nutrient medium, very moist to wet soils that are often associated with water-receiving (floodplains) and water-collecting (marshes, fens) sites. These site conditions develop under boreal, wet-temperate, and cool-mesothermal climatic regimes. Associated species often include field horsetail (*Equisetum arvense* L.), and common red sphagnum (*Sphagnum capillaceum* [Weiss] Schrank). In forest habitats, bluejoint grass prefers very moist to wet soils but can tolerate imperfectly

to moderately well-drained soils and, once established, is drought-tolerant. It is found predominantly on fine-textured soils with good water-holding capacity and on sandy soils with high water tables. Preferred soils are moderately rich in nitrogen and have an optimum pH range of 5.0–5.9. Although bluejoint grass is a shade-tolerant/intolerant species, it does best in open sites, where it often forms a distinctive tall herb layer under aspen–spruce or aspen stands. In west-central Alberta, a moderate cover of bluejoint grass is indicative of productive spruce sites. In wetland habitats in the southern part of the Boreal Forest Region in northern Ontario, this species is associated with seepage areas in cedar swamps having well-decomposed organic soils.

Bluejoint grass is a significant competitor with crop trees throughout the Boreal Forest Region. After fires, it colonizes moist to wet sites and is typically abundant within weeks after burning. Colonization may be from surviving rhizomes, which increase in abundance after burning, or by the rapid seeding-in of burned sites, provided that a suitable seed source is available. Rapid colonization of disturbed sites reduces soil erosion and nutrient loss but it also results in severe competition for spruce regeneration, especially on moist, nutrient rich sites. On these sites, bluejoint grass roots in the same soil zone as young tree seedlings, producing a very dense, continuous sod that reduces tree growth. It can also shade out young seedlings, and its heavy litter causes snow-press damage and smothering. Mechanical or chemical control is often undertaken during crop seedling establishment to ensure an adequate survival rate of conifers.

Distribution and Habitat

Distribution: Transcontinental. Bluejoint grass is a variable species in terms of plant size, panicle size and shape, and coloration; it is represented by several varieties across Canada.

Bluejoint Grass
Calamagrostide du Canada

Habitat: Most commonly found in wet to moist habitats, such as wetlands, wet thickets, shorelines, streambanks, and ditches; also in open woods, meadows, and, less frequently, on dry shallow soils and rock outcrops.

Description

General: Large, robust grass, 50–150 cm tall, arising from creeping rhizomes and often forming extensive swards; stems often purplish at the nodes, thus the name "bluejoint" grass.

Leaves: Long, flat, gradually tapering to a point, 4–8 mm wide; rough to the touch on both surfaces and on the margins; bluish-green; ligule long, membranous, with a ragged tip.

Inflorescence: Large, open to dense, occasionally drooping, often purple-tinged panicle **(a)**, with many spikelets along each branch; spikelets **(b)** one-flowered; each floret with a tuft of hairs at the base, about as long as the floret; glumes persist on the branch after the seed drops.

Phenology: Flowering takes place between June and August; seed set occurs from mid-August to late September.

a

b

1 cm

1 mm

> *Notes* Bluejoint grass is of low to moderate importance as a food source for wildlife. It is often a significant component of "beaver grass", which is harvested from wet, natural meadows to feed domestic livestock.

Circaea alpina L.
Onagraceae (Evening-Primrose Family)

Indicator Value/Significance to Forest Management

Dwarf enchanter's-nightshade is a shade-tolerant herb characteristic of moist forests and a good indicator of nutrient rich, moist soils. It occurs on water-receiving sites in association with closed canopy, coniferous and deciduous forest types under boreal, cool-temperate, and cool-mesothermal climatic regimes. In British Columbia, its frequency of occurrence increases with increasing continentality. In eastern North America, dwarf enchanter's-nightshade is characteristic of wet, seepage areas under upland balsam fir and black spruce, where it occupies patches of mineral soil on the moss-dominated forest floor.

	Poor	Medium	Rich
Wet			
Moist			▓
Fresh			
Dry			

Other species having similar indicator values include western skunk cabbage, naked mitrewort, devil's club, and electrified cat's tail moss (*Rhytidiadelphus triquetrus* (Hedw.) Warnst.). Dwarf enchanter's-nightshade is a delicate, insect-pollinated forest herb which contributes to the balsam fir–black spruce forest ecosystem by increasing biodiversity in a typically species-poor habitat.

Distribution and Habitat

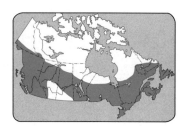

Distribution: British Columbia, southeastern Yukon, and adjacent Northwest Territories, east throughout the Boreal Forest Region of northern Alberta and Saskatchewan to southern Labrador and Newfoundland. Slightly larger plants found in southern British Columbia and on the Queen Charlotte Islands have been recognized as a separate subspecies, spp. *pacifica* (Asch. & Magnus) Raven. Dwarf enchanter's-nightshade has been designated as a rare species in the Yukon and continental Northwest Territories; in the United States, it is rare in Illinois and Iowa.

Habitat: Moist places, bare organic or moss-covered depressions, and on moss-covered rocks and peatlands in cold temperate and boreal forests.

Dwarf Enchanter's-Nightshade
Circée alpine

Description

General: Delicate herb, 10–30 cm tall, arising from a thickened, tuberous rhizome; with a simple or few-branched green stem, occasionally purple at the nodes.

Leaves: Opposite; 2–5 pairs on the stem; ovate to heart-shaped, 2–5 cm long, upper leaves largest; margins coarsely toothed; pale green, translucent.

Flowers: Small, with 2 notched white petals, 1–2 mm long; 8–12 flowers forming a terminal raceme up to 10 cm long.

Fruit: Ovoid to club-shaped capsule, 2–3 mm long, covered with soft, hooked bristles, and containing 1 seed.

Phenology: Flowers bloom from June to August, rarely into early September; the fruit matures in late summer or early fall.

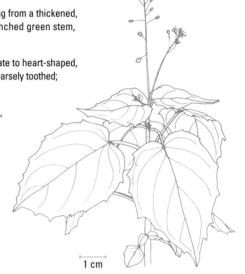

1 cm

Coptis trifolia (L.) Salisb.
Ranunculaceae (Buttercup Family)

Indicator Value/Significance to Forest Management

Goldthread is a shade-tolerant/intolerant herb that is a good indicator of nutrient poor to nutrient medium, moist to wet soils having moderately low pH levels and moderately low levels of available nitrogen. These soils are often mineral gleysolic or organic, typically developing under boreal, cool-temperate, and cool-mesothermal climatic regimes. Goldthread occurs in a broad range of habitats, but is most frequently encountered in moist to wet, coniferous forests on water-receiving sites. Goldthread shows high regional presence values for both white spruce–

	Poor	Medium	Rich
Wet	■	■	
Moist	■	■	
Fresh			
Dry			

balsam fir and black spruce stands in the Boreal Forest Region in eastern and Atlantic Canada. In wet habitats of the Boreal Forest Region in Ontario, including the Northern Clay Section, this species is indicative of minerotrophy in shrub rich, treed bogs with undecomposed organic soils and a near-surface water table. In upland hardwood ecosystems of the Great Lakes–St. Lawrence Forest Region, this species is indicative of moist, very infertile soils supporting stands dominated by hemlock and other conifers; on these sites it is highly associated with thick, raw, acidic humus. Other species with similar indicator values include cinnamon fern (*Osmunda cinnamomea* L.), interrupted fern, and the liverwort *Bazzania trilobata* (L.) S.F. Gray.

Distribution and Habitat

Distribution: Coastal British Columbia, foothills of central Alberta, east to Labrador and Newfoundland.

Habitat: Moist coniferous forests and thickets, mossy places, sometimes on well-decayed, moss-covered logs.

Goldthread
Savoyane

Description

General: Small, stemless, perennial herb arising from a slender, bright yellow rhizome; with long-stalked, basal leaves and slender, leafless, flowering stalks.

Leaves: Evergreen, persistent through the winter; basal, long-stalked, divided into 3 obscurely lobed and sharply toothed leaflets; dark green and lustrous above, paler below.

Flowers: Solitary on a long, slender stalk, 3–15 cm tall; star-shaped, 1–1.5 cm across, with 5–7 petal-like, white to pinkish sepals; true petals small, yellow, fleshy, and modified into nectaries.

Fruit: Follicles, 3–6 on separate stalks at the top of the flower stalk, spreading at maturity, tipped with long straight beaks, each containing a few large, glossy, black seeds.

Phenology: Flowers bloom in late May to early June; the fruit appears in July and August.

Synonym: *Coptis groenlandica* (Oeder) Fern.

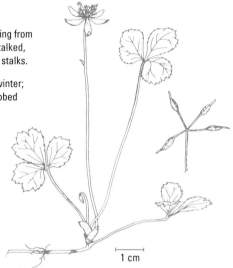

1 cm

Notes   A yellow dye can be made from the rhizome.

Herbs and Grasses

Cypripedium acaule Ait.
Orchidaceae (Orchid Family)

Indicator Value/Significance to Forest Management

Moccasin flower is a shade-tolerant/intolerant, oxylophytic orchid found primarily on nutrient poor, dry to fresh, sandy and coarse loamy soils in dry woods and on sand dunes; it also occurs on acidic soils adjacent to swamps and bogs. It is occasional to locally common in jack pine and black spruce stands in the Boreal Forest Region. In the Great Lakes– St. Lawrence Forest Region, it is characteristic of white pine stands. Species with similar indicator values include mayflower and wintergreen (*Gaultheria procumbens* L.). Moccasin flower

sometimes forms large colonies that can benefit the sterile, coarsely textured soils it grows on by adding nutrient rich, organic matter through annual dieback; this enhances the soil moisture regime and cation-exchange capacity. Moccasin flower also contributes to species richness in forest stands that are typically species poor; it is insect-pollinated, thus providing food resources for insect populations.

Distribution and Habitat

Distribution: Lake Athabasca in northeastern Alberta, northern Saskatchewan, east through Manitoba to the Maritimes and Newfoundland. Moccasin flower is designated as a rare species in Alberta; in the United States, it is rare in Illinois and Rhode Island, endangered in Vermont, and threatened in Alabama.

Habitat: Sterile, acidic soils in a variety of habitats, including dry coniferous forests, dry open hardwood stands, and sphagnum bogs under a cover of black spruce and tamarack, where it occupies the tops of hummocks and other drier areas.

Moccasin Flower • Pink Lady's-Slipper
Cypripède acaule

Description

General: Perennial herb, 15–40 cm tall, arising from a short underground rhizome; having 2 large basal leaves and a single large showy pink flower; sometimes forming large colonies.

Leaves: Two large basal leaves; each 10–20 cm long, narrowly oblong-elliptic; strongly ribbed with parallel veins; sparsely hairy; green above, shiny-silvery green below.

Flowers: Solitary; nodding, showy, sub-tended by a leaf-like bract over-arching the flower; lateral petals and sepals linear, yellowish-green to brown; floral lip an inflated, obovoid pouch, crimson pink (very rarely white), with branching dark purple veining, fissured in front with edges folded in and downward.

1 cm

Fruit: Brown seed capsule, erect, strongly ribbed, 3–4.5 cm long, containing numerous, tiny seeds.

Phenology: Flower blooms in spring from May to late June or, in cold exposed habitats, as late as early July; the seeds mature in late summer or early fall.

Notes Moccasin flower is difficult to transplant and cultivate, and is not recommended for garden culture. It has been reported that handling the plant can result in dermatitis.

Elymus innovatus Beal
Poaceae (Grass Family)

Indicator Value/Significance to Forest Management

Hairy wild rye is a shade-intolerant grass characteristic of moderately nutrient rich to nutrient rich soils with dry to fresh soil moisture regimes and rocky to sandy textures. It is very common in open woodlands, especially in open pine, spruce, and aspen forests, from western Manitoba to western Alberta. It often occurs in association with bearberry and soapberry. This species shows moderate regional presence value for boreal white spruce−balsam fir stands from

northern British Columbia to central Manitoba. Hairy wild rye is a sod-forming grass noted for its deep, spreading root system and production of tillers, which make it an important species for stabilizing exposed sandy soils.

Distribution and Habitat

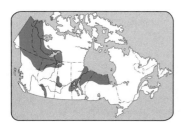

Distribution: Yukon and western Northwest Territories, northern British Columbia and Alberta, southern foothills of Alberta, northwestern corner of Saskatchewan around Lake Athabasca, west-central Saskatchewan, central Manitoba northeast to the Hudson Bay coast, and northern Ontario along major rivers flowing into Hudson Bay and James Bay.

Habitat: Boreal forest habitats, parkland, and mixedwood forests, clearings and openings; on calcareous, sandy and shaly soils; uncommon on the prairies.

Hairy Wild Rye
Élyme innovant

Description

General: Coarse, perennial grass, 30–100 cm tall, arising in tufts from a long, creeping rhizome; with flat to involute leaves and slender elongated spikes.

Leaves: Firm, 2–5 mm wide, flat or involute on drying, rough to touch on both sides.

Inflorescence: A spike **(a)**, 5–12 cm long, spikelets densely packed, with 2 spikelets at each node; spikelets 10–15 mm long, with long straight hairs; lemmas about 10 mm long, with a short awn 2–4 mm long; glumes 10–12 mm long, purplish or grayish, densely hairy.

Phenology: Flowers bloom in June and July; the seeds mature from late July to September.

a

1 cm

1 cm

Epilobium angustifolium L.
Onagraceae (Evening-Primrose Family)

Indicator Value/Significance to Forest Management

Fireweed is a shade-intolerant, nitrophytic herb that is a good indicator of nutrient medium, dry to fresh soils. It characteristically grows in recently burned areas and cutovers on a wide variety of sites, where it indicates increased decomposition of the forest floor materials (typically mor humus forms). Fireweed is often associated with hair cap moss (*Polytrichum juniperinum* Hedw.). It tends to be frequently associated with black spruce and balsam fir stands in western portions of the Boreal Forest Region, less so in eastern Canada.

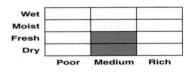

	Poor	Medium	Rich
Wet			
Moist			
Fresh		■	
Dry			

In the earliest stages of stand development, fireweed is an important competitor for coniferous crop species. However, as a pioneer of recently disturbed areas, it cannot invade sites with standing vegetation. Mechanical site preparation decreases competition from other species, but provides a suitable seedbed for fireweed. High density stands of fireweed may hinder survival and growth of young forest plantations by shading tree seedlings and reducing ground temperatures. Such shading is usually only a temporary problem since fireweed degenerates annually and must resprout from ground level each spring. Although fireweed colonies may hinder the growth of conifer tree seedlings, they cause relatively few mortalities. Fireweed's extensive root system helps to bind soils and reduce erosion. After fire, fireweed takes up available nutrients and quickly recycles them through its own dead and decaying plant parts. Fireweed cover may also delay the development of shrubby vegetation on cleared or burned areas, thereby assisting coniferous species in becoming established before competing shrubs.

Distribution and Habitat

Distribution: Circumpolar; occurring throughout Canada from sea level to subalpine elevations.

Habitat: A successional, shade-intolerant species commonly found in open areas; recently burned sites, roadsides, clearings and disturbed ground; mostly on sandy, loamy, and fine-textured soils, with dry to fresh moisture conditions.

Fireweed
Épilobe à feuilles étroites

Description

General: Perennial herb, 10–200 cm tall, arising from a rhizome; stems erect, usually unbranched; the rhizome system persists for many years, producing aerial shoots annually in late March to early June.

Leaves: Alternate; narrowly lanceolate, 3–20 cm long; margin smooth to slightly toothed; expanding most rapidly between April and mid-June.

Flowers: Clustered in a conspicuous terminal spike, with the lowest flowers in the spike blooming first; individual flowers large, about 2 cm across; with 4 magenta to pink (rarely white), showy petals and a long exerted stigma divided into 4 reflexed lobes.

Fruit: Long (5–8 cm), narrow capsule, opening to release numerous silky-haired seeds; seeds develop and are released from the bottom of the spike as flowers continue to bloom at the top.

Phenology: The flowering season extends from June to September; the flowers bloom progressively from the bottom to the top of the inflorescence throughout the summer, producing flowers at the tip long after the basal seeds have ripened and dispersed.

1 cm

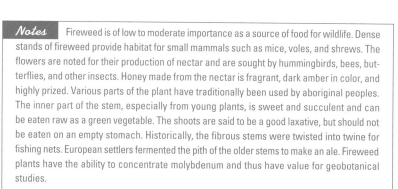

Notes   Fireweed is of low to moderate importance as a source of food for wildlife. Dense stands of fireweed provide habitat for small mammals such as mice, voles, and shrews. The flowers are noted for their production of nectar and are sought by hummingbirds, bees, butterflies, and other insects. Honey made from the nectar is fragrant, dark amber in color, and highly prized. Various parts of the plant have traditionally been used by aboriginal peoples. The inner part of the stem, especially from young plants, is sweet and succulent and can be eaten raw as a green vegetable. The shoots are said to be a good laxative, but should not be eaten on an empty stomach. Historically, the fibrous stems were twisted into twine for fishing nets. European settlers fermented the pith of the older stems to make an ale. Fireweed plants have the ability to concentrate molybdenum and thus have value for geobotanical studies.

Erythronium americanum Ker
Liliaceae (Lily Family)

Indicator Value/Significance to Forest Management

Trout lily is a shade-intolerant herb characteristic of nutrient medium to rich, well-drained, moist, sandy loam soils, with slightly acidic to neutral pH and supporting the development of moder and mull humus forms. This species occurs in eastern beech and sugar maple forests, also in thickets along streams and in clearings. Trout lily is commonly associated with spinulose wood fern, common wood-sorrel, wild ginger, wild lily-of-the-valley (*Maianthemum canadense* Desf.), spring beauty (*Claytonia caroliniana* Michx.),and purple trillium (*Trillium erectum* L.). It

is one of the spring ephemeral species associated with eastern tolerant hardwood forests. Spring ephemeral species appear before leaf emergence of the canopy-forming trees or shrubs, completing their life cycles before most ground layer species have emerged. Although trout lily is a diminutive plant, producing only 2 leaves at most, it is a colonial species that often covers much of the forest floor in early spring. It benefits the forest community by increasing nutrient cycling through deposition of nutrient rich litter, and by enhancing the soil moisture regime and cation-exchange capacity by adding organic matter. Root development and shoot elongation extend through the winter months in preparation for a rapid spring emergence, thus tending to mix and loosen soil particles and lessen soil compaction. The temporal separation between spring ephemeral species, such as trout lily, and those summer green and evergreen species that occupy the same microsites later in the season, adds another dimension to the biodiversity of the forest ecosystem; trout lily also provides food resources for insects in early spring.

Distribution and Habitat

Distribution: Northeastern shore of Lake Superior in Ontario, east to Quebec, New Brunswick, and Nova Scotia.

Habitat: Rich woods, hardwood forests, and thickets.

Trout Lily • Yellow Dog's-Tooth • Yellow Adder's-Tongue
Érythrone d'Amérique

Description

General: Perennial woodland lily arising from
a deeply buried, solid bulb; with large, solitary,
yellow, nodding flowers and 2 apparently basal
leaves; forming colonies of 1-leaved young,
sterile plants and 2-leaved fertile ones.

Leaves: Essentially basal, 2, smooth, often mottled; lanceolate to elliptic, tapering to the base and
sheathing the stem; the larger leaves 2–5 cm wide.

Flowers: Solitary, nodding, lily-like; 1.8–4 cm long; the
3 petals and 3 sepals similar, spreading and recurved,
yellow, often spotted near the base; on a long stalk
5–20 cm long.

Fruit: Oval-shaped capsule, contracted at the base,
with 3 valves containing numerous seeds.

Phenology: The plant completes its entire life cycle in the
4–6 week period between snowmelt and leaf-out of the canopy
trees; in Canada, this period generally occurs from April to May.

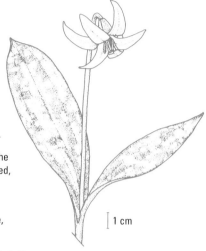

1 cm

Notes The leaves of trout lily are occasionally used as a potherb, and the small bulbs
are nutritious and sweet, but difficult to dig. The species may be of value medicinally, but
this is yet unproven.

Galium triflorum Michx.
Rubiaceae (Madder Family)

Indicator Value/Significance to Forest Management

Sweet-scented bedstraw is a shade-tolerant, nitrophytic species characteristic of nutrient rich, fresh to very moist soils that develop under boreal, temperate, and cool-mesothermal climates. It commonly occurs on water-receiving sites (alluvial, floodplain, seepage areas, streambanks) in early-seral forest communities. In mountainous areas, its frequency of occurrence decreases with increasing elevation. In the Boreal Forest Region, sweet-scented bedstraw shows a high regional presence value for white spruce–balsam fir stands, from northwestern Alberta to

western Quebec, and sporadic occurrence in black spruce stands from central Alberta to northern Ontario. In wetland habitats in the southern Boreal Forest Region in Ontario, it is associated with hardwood swamps on alluvial sites having neutral to slightly basic, nutrient rich, silt and clay-textured soils. Associated species include lady fern, sword fern, thimbleberry, and three-leaved foamflower.

Distribution and Habitat

Distribution: Southern Yukon and British Columbia, east to southern Labrador and Newfoundland. Sweet-scented bedstraw has been designated as a rare species in the Yukon and continental Northwest Territories.

Habitat: Occurs across a range of forest habitats on fresh to moist soil/site conditions.

Sweet-Scented Bedstraw
Gaillet à trois fleurs

Description

General: Slender, trailing, perennial herb, with square stems, whorled leaves, and tiny flowers in few-flowered clusters; prostrate or clinging to other vegetation with numerous, small, hooked bristles.

Leaves: In whorls of 6; broadly lanceolate to oblanceolate, with small sharp-pointed tips; margin and lower surface rough to touch.

Flowers: In loose, 3-flowered clusters on long stalks from the leaf axils; individual flowers tiny, about 3 mm across; corolla 4-lobed, greenish-white.

Fruit: A pair of small, fused, globular capsules, about 2 mm across; densely bristly with hooked hairs.

Phenology: Flowers bloom in June; the fruit matures in August.

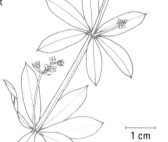

1 cm

Notes Sweet-scented bedstraw contains coumarin, which indirectly inhibits the blood-clotting process. Coumarin has a characteristic vanilla-like odor and the dried plants were once widely used for freshening bedding.

Laportea canadensis (L.) Wedd.
Urticaceae (Nettle Family)

Indicator Value/Significance to Forest Management

Wood nettle is a shade-tolerant herb that is a good indicator of nitrogen rich, moist to wet soils with mull humus forms. It occurs on water-receiving sites, where it is common in rich, sugar maple stands, moist woods, and on

	Poor	Medium	Rich
Wet			■
Moist			■
Fresh			
Dry			

wooded streambanks. In the northern hardwoods of Quebec, this species is characteristic of white elm−sugar maple and white elm−black ash stands on moist, bottomland alluvial soils. Common species associates include blue cohosh (*Caulophyllum thalictroides* [L.] Michx.), spotted touch-me-not (*Impatiens capensis* Meerb.), and sensitive fern.

Distribution and Habitat

Distribution: Southeastern Saskatchewan, southern Manitoba, Ontario, east to New Brunswick and Nova Scotia. Wood nettle has been designated as a rare species in Saskatchewan and Prince Edward Island.

Habitat: Rich, moist woods, often forming a dominant zone in mid-slope areas along streams.

Wood Nettle
Laportéa du Canada

Description

General: Perennial herb, up to 1 m tall, with an erect, often zigzagging stem covered with stinging hairs; often forming colonies.

Leaves: Alternate; long-stalked, broadly ovate, slender-tipped, 8–15 cm long; margin coarsely toothed.

Flowers: Small, several in loose, elongate, branched clusters from the leaf axils; separate male and female flowers on the same plant: female flowers, larger, mainly in clusters from the axils of the upper leaves; male flowers mainly in clusters from the lower leaf axils.

Fruit: Flat, D-shaped achenes, 3–4 mm long.

Phenology: Flowers bloom in July and August; the seeds mature between August and September.

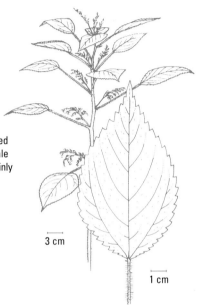

3 cm

1 cm

Lysichitum americanum Hult. & St. John
Araceae (Arum Family)

Indicator Value/Significance to Forest Management

Western skunk cabbage is a shade-tolerant/intolerant nitrophytic herb that is a good indicator of nutrient rich, mineral gleysolic and organic soils with moder and mull humus forms, and wet to very wet soil moisture regimes with slow moving groundwater close to the surface. Often these soils are very rich in mineral nutrients, particularly magnesium. This species commonly occurs on water-receiving (hillside seepage) and water-collecting sites, where it is often dominant in the ground cover under open-canopy stands of red alder, Sitka spruce, yellow-cedar, and western redcedar. Western skunk cabbage is a sensitive indicator of winter water table depth in these rich, productive habitats, and can be used, in conjunction with slough sedge (*Carex obnupta* Bail.), to identify highly productive sites. It is found within subalpine-boreal, cool-temperate, and cool-mesothermal climatic regimes. Commonly associated species with similar indicator values include lady fern, sword fern, thimbleberry, three-leaved foamflower, field horse-tail (*Equisetum arvense* L.), the moss *Kindbergia praelonga* (Hedw.) Ochyra, and the liverwort *Pellia neesiana* (Gott.) Limpr.

	Poor	Medium	Rich
Wet			
Moist			
Fresh			
Dry			

Distribution and Habitat

Distribution: Coastal British Columbia, east to the Columbia River valley in the southeastern part of the province.

Habitat: Swamps and wet woods.

Western Skunk Cabbage
Lysichiton d'Amérique

Description

General: Perennial herb with large, basal, simple leaves; arising from a short, fleshy, upright, underground rhizome; entire plant has a strong skunk-like odor when bruised or crushed.

Leaves: In a basal cluster; large, up to 100 cm long, oblong to elliptic.

Flowers: Numerous, small, greenish-yellow flowers, borne on a fleshy, cylindrical spadix; spadix surrounded by a nearly sessile, yellow, leaf-like spathe, up to 20 cm long.

Fruit: Small berries, clustered on the spadix, each with 1–2 seeds.

Phenology: Flowers bloom from April to July, sometimes earlier when the snow melts.

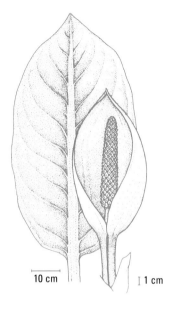

10 cm   1 cm

Notes   The berries, reported to be eaten by squirrels and bears, are said to have a very acrid and pungent taste. The young leaves, flowers, stalks, and roots have been sparingly used by some aboriginal peoples, but consumption is not recommended. The plants contain long, sharp crystals of calcium oxalate, which when eaten, become embedded in mucous membranes and cause intense irritation and burning. Prolonged cooking and storage eliminates the crystals, thus removing the burning sensation. Roasted roots can be ground into flour. The thick, waxy leaves were often used by aboriginal peoples as "wax paper" for lining berry baskets, berry-drying racks, and steaming pits.

Mitella nuda L.
Saxifragaceae (Saxifrage Family)

Indicator Value/Significance to Forest Management

Naked mitrewort is a shade-tolerant/intolerant herb characteristic of nutrient medium to nutrient rich soils with neutral to high pH levels and fresh to moist soil moisture regimes. Soils supporting this species typically have moder and mull humus forms and are developed under continental, boreal, and cool-temperate climates. Naked mitrewort is infrequent to common on water-shedding and water-receiving sites in the sparse understory communities of cool, continental, coniferous forests. In British Columbia, its frequency of occurrence increases with increasing elevation

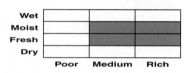

	Poor	Medium	Rich
Wet			
Moist			
Fresh			
Dry			

and continentality. In the Boreal Forest Region, naked mitrewort shows high regional presence values for white spruce–balsam fir stands across Canada, but is absent or infrequent in black spruce stands east of Ontario. In wetland habitats in the southern section of the Boreal Forest Region in Ontario, and in the western part of the Great Lakes–St. Lawrence Forest Region, it is associated with seepage areas in cedar swamps having well-decomposed peaty soils. Associated species with similar indicator values include lady fern, dwarf enchanter's-nightshade, red-osier dogwood, devil's club, and electrified cat's tail moss (*Rhytidiadelphus triquetrus* [Hedw.] Warnst.). This delicate herb increases the species richness of forest sites.

Distribution and Habitat

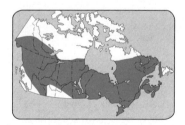

Distribution: Southern Yukon and British Columbia, east to Labrador and western Newfoundland. Naked mitrewort has been designated as a rare species in the Yukon. In the United States, it is rare in Connecticut.

Habitat: Cool, wet coniferous forests.

Naked Mitrewort
Mitrelle nue

Description

General: Low, creeping, perennial herb, with basal leaves and a solitary, erect, flowering stem, up to 20 cm tall; spreading by both rhizomes and runners.

Leaves: Basal; long-stalked; round to kidney-shaped, 3–5 cm long; margins shallowly lobed and crenate; sparsely long hairy on the upper surface and along the stalk.

Flowers: Borne in a sparse, spike-like inflorescence **(a)**; individual flowers **(b)** about 1 cm across, saucer-shaped, with 5, feathery, pinnately-divided, greenish petals.

Fruit: Short, beaked capsule; at maturity splitting into 2 parts to release a few, black, smooth, shiny seeds.

Phenology: Flowers bloom in May and June; the seeds ripen in July and August.

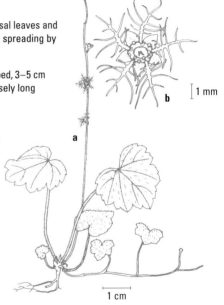

b ⌉ 1 mm

a

1 cm

Moneses uniflora (L.) A. Gray
Pyrolaceae (Wintergreen Family)

Indicator Value/Significance to Forest Management

One-flowered pyrola is a shade-tolerant herb characteristic of nutrient medium, fresh to moist soils that are often rich in mycorrhiza and have mor and acidic moder humus. These soils are typically associated with boreal, wet-temperate, and cool-mesothermal climatic regimes. This species is infrequent to locally common on water-shedding and water-receiving sites in partially open to dense, cool, mossy, coniferous forests. In British Columbia, its frequency of occurrence increases with increasing precipitation and decreases with increasing eleva-

tion. In southwestern Alberta, one-flowered pyrola is one of a small group of herb species, also including queen's cup (*Clintonia uniflora* [Schult.]) Kunth), five-stamened mitrewort (*Mitella pentandra* Hook.), one-leaved foamflower (*Tiarella unifoliata* Hook.), one-flowered globeflower (*Trollius laxus* Salisb. var. *albiflorus* A. Gray), and lesser pyrola (*Pyrola minor* L.), that indicates the limits of spruce–fir stands. In the Boreal Forest Region, one-flowered pyrola shows a high regional presence value for white spruce–balsam fir stands throughout the region, but is infrequent or absent in black spruce stands. This species is a diminutive plant that usually forms small colonies. Its presence contributes to forest biodiversity and its flowers provide food resources for the insects that pollinate them.

Distribution and Habitat

Distribution: Yukon and British Columbia, east to Labrador and Newfoundland, absent only in the tundra regions of northern Canada and on the prairies of southern Alberta and Saskatchewan.

Habitat: Growing on moist, moss mats in mainly coniferous forests.

One-Flowered Pyrola • One-Flowered Wintergreen
Monésès uniflore

Description

General: Low, perennial, evergreen herb, with essentially basal leaves and a single flowering stem about 10 cm tall; spreading by rhizomes, often forming small colonies.

Leaves: An apparently basal rosette of 3–4 leaves on a very short stem; each leaf with a short stalk, usually shorter than the small, oval-shaped, leathery blades; margins wavy-toothed.

Flowers: Solitary and nodding on a leafless stalk; white, 1–2 cm across, with 5 waxy petals, fragrant; style straight, with a castle-like knob on the end; flowers change from nodding to erect as the seeds mature.

Fruit: Round, brown, erect capsule with a protruding style, filled with numerous small seeds.

Phenology: Flowers bloom from mid-June to August; the seeds reach maturity in late August.

1 cm

Oxalis montana Raf.
Oxalidaceae (Wood-Sorrel Family)

Indicator Value/Significance to Forest Management

Common wood-sorrel is a shade-tolerant herb that is a good indicator of fresh to moist, nutrient medium to nutrient rich, subacidic soils. It occurs on water-receiving sites in boreal coniferous and mixed forests, and on upper water-shedding sites in hardwood forests. Common wood-sorrel shows high regional presence value for boreal white spruce stands from the west end of Lake Superior to Cape Breton, but is absent or infrequent in black spruce stands. In the eastern sections of the Great Lakes–St. Lawrence Forest Region, its occurrence on lower slopes indi-

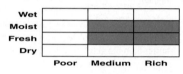

cates site characteristics suitable for good production of balsam fir (*Abies balsamea* [L.] Mill.); on upper slopes, its occurrence indicates sites where good growth of hardwood species can be expected. Species with similar indicator values include bluebead lily (*Clintonia borealis* (Ait.) Raf.), spinulose wood fern, and wild lily-of-the-valley (*Maianthemum canadense* Desf.).

Distribution and Habitat

Distribution: Ontario, east through Quebec, the Maritimes, Labrador and Newfoundland. Common wood-sorrel has been designated as a rare species in Newfoundland.

Habitat: Rich, moist woods.

Common Wood-Sorrel
Oxalide de montagne

Description

General: Low, perennial herb with basal leaves and white flowers arising from a slender rhizome.

Leaves: Few, basal, long-stalked, divided into 3 clover-like leaflets; each leaflet 1.3–3 cm wide, softly hairy; exhibiting diurnal movement: at night, they droop downwards so that their undersurfaces face each other; during the day, they are normally extended unless exposed to direct sunlight, which will cause them to droop downwards again.

Flowers: Solitary; on long stalks 6–15 cm long, slightly taller than the leaves, with 2 small bracts above the middle; petals white, veined with pink, notched at the tips, 10–15 mm long.

Fruit: Cylindrical capsule, 4–5 sided in cross-section, containing numerous seeds, 1–2 mm long.

Phenology: Flowers bloom between late May and August; the seeds mature in July and August.

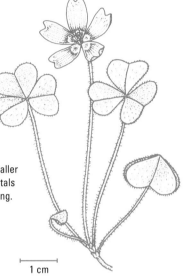

1 cm

Smilacina racemosa (L.) Desf.
Liliaceae (Lily Family)

Indicator Value/Significance to Forest Management

False spikenard is a shade-tolerant, nitrophytic herb characteristic of nutrient medium to nutrient rich, fresh to moist soils with moder and mull humus forms. This species is scattered to plentiful on water-shedding sites, and plentiful on water-receiving sites, particularly on floodplains in association with deciduous forests. In British Columbia, it is found in submontane to subalpine habitats in cool-temperate and cool-mesothermal climates. Here it is common in aspen–hazelnut ecosystems, often occurring with Rocky Mountain maple (*Acer glabrum* Torr.),

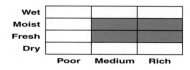

Hooker's fairybells (*Disporum hookeri* [Torr.] Nicholson), mountain sweet cicely (*Osmorhiza chilensis* Hook. & Arnott), sword fern, black cottonwood, and three-leaved foamflower. In upland hardwood–hemlock stands in the Great Lakes–St. Lawrence Forest Region in eastern Ontario, false spikenard is indicative of moist, fertile to very fertile soils. Here it is strongly associated with leatherwood, hairy Solomon's-seal (*Polygonatum pubescens* [Willd.] Pursh), and Selkirk's violet (*Viola selkirkii* Pursh ex J. Goldie). In the northern hardwoods of Quebec, it is characteristic of sugar maple associations growing on knolls and moderately deep till slopes. However, in the Rainy River Section of the Great Lakes–St. Lawrence Forest Region, the species is absent from fresh sites and is considered to have little indicator value.

False spikenard often forms extensive colonies consisting of closely spaced, large, leafy stems which can limit the availability of site resources to germinants and newly planted crop tree seedlings through direct competition for light, soil moisture and nutrients, and rooting space. This species helps to improve site conditions by reducing nutrient losses due to soil leaching and by adding organic matter to the soil through leaf fall.

Distribution and Habitat

Distribution: Two varieties occur in Canada. The western variety *amplexicaulis* (Nutt.) S. Wats., with sessile, clasping, acute-tipped leaves, occurs from British Columbia east to Saskatchewan. The eastern variety *racemosa*, with short-stalked, more pointed leaves, occurs from southeastern Manitoba east to the Maritimes and western Newfoundland. False spikenard has been designated as a rare species in Saskatchewan, Manitoba, and Newfoundland.

Habitat: Rich, shaded forests, thickets, and clearings.

False Spikenard
Smilacine à grappes

Description

General: Perennial herb arising from a long, stout, creeping rhizome; stems erect or curved-ascending, slightly zigzagging, bearing few to many leaves and a terminal cluster of flowers.

Leaves: Alternate; sessile or nearly so; spreading horizontally in 2 rows; elliptic, with a tapering tip and rounded base, 7–15 cm long, 2–7 cm wide; hairy on the lower surface.

Flowers: In many-flowered, terminal, cylindrical cluster; individual flowers small, 3–5 mm across, with 6 white petals.

Fruit: Globular berry, red with purple mottling, containing 1–2 seeds.

Phenology: Flowers bloom in May and June.

Synonym: *Maianthemum racemosum* (L.) Link ssp. *racemosum*.

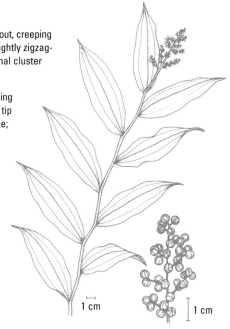

1 cm

1 cm

Notes   The berries of false spikenard are edible but not palatable. Plants are easily transplanted and make attractive ornamentals in shaded gardens.

Tiarella trifoliata L.
Saxifragaceae (Saxifrage Family)

Indicator Value/Significance to Forest Management

Three-leaved foamflower is a shade-tolerant/intolerant nitrophytic herb that is a good indicator for nutrient rich, fresh to very moist but strongly drained soils often characterized by moder and mull humus forms. This species indicates base-rich parent materials that are capable of compensating for the rapid removal of soil nutrients by drainage water. Three-leaved foamflower grows under a hypermaritime, cool-mesothermal climatic regime in the Coast Forest Region of British Columbia. It occurs on water-receiving sites (typically seepage areas), where it

	Poor	Medium	Rich
Wet			
Moist			▓
Fresh			▓
Dry			

is scattered to abundant in productive stands of Douglas-fir, Sitka spruce, and western redcedar. This species is also found in devil's club−oak fern and devil's club−lady fern ecosystems in coastal and interior regions. Its frequency of occurrence decreases with increasing latitude, elevation, and continentality. Common associates include vanilla leaf, lady fern, sweet-scented bedstraw, sword fern, thimbleberry, and salmonberry.

Distribution and Habitat

Distribution: Coastal British Columbia, inland through central and southern British Columbia to western Alberta. Three-leaved foamflower has been designated as a rare species in Alberta.

Habitat: Moist, shady forest habitats, especially along streambanks.

Three-Leaved Foamflower
Tiarelle trifoliée

Description

General: Perennial herb, 15–40 cm tall, arising from a rhizome; with compound, basal leaves and a flowering stem bearing a terminal, elongated cluster of flowers; stem hairy with gland-tipped hairs.

Leaves: Basal leaves long-stalked, composed of 3 sharply toothed leaflets, the terminal leaflet shallowly 3-lobed; stem leaves few, similar to the basal ones but shorter-stalked.

Flowers: Numerous, clustered in an open, elongated, terminal inflorescence; individual flowers **(a)** tiny, with narrow, white petals and a glandular-hairy, lobed calyx.

Fruit: A capsule **(b)** containing few seeds.

Phenology: Flowers bloom from April to July.

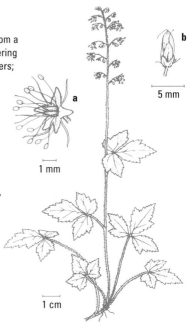

b

5 mm

a

1 mm

1 cm

Trillium cernuum L.
Liliaceae (Lily Family)

Indicator Value/Significance to Forest Management

Nodding trillium is a shade-tolerant herb characteristic of nitrogen rich, fine-textured, fresh to moist soils. This species is associated with rich, deciduous sugar maple, balsam poplar, aspen, and black ash forests, as well as mixedwoods and, to a lesser extent, thickets. In upland northern hardwood–hemlock forest ecosystems in the Great Lakes–St. Lawrence Forest Region, nodding trillium is characteristic of fresh to very moist, fertile soils in shaded locations. It is absent in both dry and very wet habitats. In the white spruce–balsam fir–yellow birch forests of

	Poor	Medium	Rich
Wet			
Moist			▓
Fresh			▓
Dry			

Quebec, it is considered to be a good indicator of rich site conditions. Nodding trillium is seldom common where found, typically forming small colonies with widely spaced stems in dense understory vegetation. It contributes significantly to the forest floor through nutrient cycling and the deposition of rich organic matter.

Distribution and Habitat

Distribution: Eastern Saskatchewan, east to New-foundland. Nodding trillium is a designated rare species in Saskatchewan; in the United States, it has been extirpated in Illinois and is endangered in Delaware and South Dakota.

Habitat: Fresh to moist, northern hardwood and mixedwood forests, thickets.

Nodding Trillium • Birthroot
Trille penché

Description

General: Perennial herb, usually less than 25 cm tall, arising from a thick, short rhizome; the erect stem bearing a single whorl of 3 leaves and a single, large, nodding, white flower dipped under the leaves.

Leaves: In a whorl of 3 at the top of the stem; broadly ovate, tapering quickly from the middle of the leaf to a short point at the tip and a short stalk at the base.

Flowers: Solitary; on a reflexed stalk from the top of the stem, hidden under the leaf whorl; about 4 cm across, with 3 white petals bent back at the tips.

Fruit: A 6-lobed, many-seeded, red berry.

Phenology: Flowers bloom in late May and early June; the seeds ripen in late June and July.

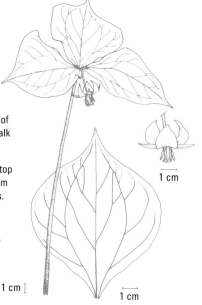

1 cm

1 cm

1 cm

Notes The leaves and rhizomes of nodding trillium are reported to have some medicinal properties. It has been used as a salve to treat skin irritations and as a drink to relieve dysentery. Aboriginal peoples made a medicine from the rhizome to aid in childbirth; the plant is sometimes known as birthroot (bethroot).

Ferns and Fern-Allies

Athyrium filix-femina (L.) Roth
Polypodiaceae (Polypody Family)

Indicator Value/Significance to Forest Management

Lady fern is a shade-tolerant, nitrophytic fern that is a good indicator of habitats having nutrient rich, very moist to wet soils, and moder and mull humus forms. These soils are usually found on water-receiving (alluvial, floodplain, seepage, stream edge) and water-collecting (swamps, marshes, fens) sites under boreal, temperate, and mesothermal climatic regimes. Sometimes lady fern forms a prominent understory in forests on very moist alluvium. Associated species with similar indicator values include dwarf enchanter's-nightshade, naked mitrewort, and electrified cat's tail moss (*Rhytidiadelphus triquetrus* [Hedw.] Warnst.). In British Columbia,

lady fern often occurs with western skunk cabbage. In the southern part of the Boreal Forest Region in Ontario, lady fern is associated with tall-shrub thicket swamps in riparian habitats having well-decomposed organic soils with some accumulation of silt. In the Great Lakes–St. Lawrence Forest Region, it shows greater ecological amplitude beneath upland hardwoods than on drier, infertile to very fertile soils on protected, cool, humid sites; on these upland sites it becomes very abundant where stands are somewhat open. Farther east, in the northern hardwood forests of Quebec, lady fern is found in sugar maple associations occurring within shallow catchment basins with wet to moist soils. On these sites it is often associated with dwarf raspberry and wild-raisin (*Viburnum cassinoides* L.).

Lady fern is not considered to be a major threat to the establishment of coniferous tree seedlings. However, because of its large size and dense stands, it has the potential to be a serious local competitor wherever it is abundant and vigorous. Smothering and mechanical damage to seedlings, caused by shedding of the fronds, is as detrimental as competition for light and space.

Distribution and Habitat

Distribution: Highly variable species with 2 subspecies recognized in Canada. Subspecies *michauxii* (Spreng.) Farw., with the blade twice as long as the stalk and with indusia kidney- to horseshoe-shaped, occurs from Manitoba east to Newfoundland. Subspecies *cyclosorum* (Ledeb.) Moore, with the blade 3 times as long as the stalk and with nearly round indusia, occurs in the Rocky Mountains from the Yukon and British Columbia as well as disjunctly

Lady Fern
Athyrium fougère-femelle

in the Gulf of St. Lawrence region in the Gaspé Peninsula and Newfoundland. Subspecies *michauxii* has been designated as a rare species in Saskatchewan; subspecies *cyclosorum* has rare status in the Yukon and continental Northwest Territories.

Habitat: Common in fresh to moist, semi-shaded woods, thickets, streambanks, swamps, and meadows.

Description

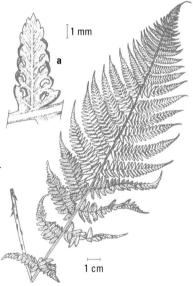

| 1 mm

a

General: Medium to large, showy, delicate woodland fern; perennial; fronds growing in a circular cluster from a thick, scaly rhizome.

Fronds: Twice-divided (bipinnate); lanceolate-elliptic, widest near the middle, 10–35 cm wide, tapering at both ends; smooth; up to 110 cm tall, with a short stalk, scaly at the base.

Reproductive Structures: Spores produced in sori on the undersides of the pinnules **(a)**; sori curved (kidney-shaped), attached along the side, located near the end of short, forked veins.

Phenology: Spores mature towards the end of the growing season, in late July, although variations in the development of the individual fronds ensure that spore dispersal is spread over a lengthy period.

├──┤
1 cm

Notes   The young shoots, or "fiddleheads", are steamed and eaten by aboriginal peoples in British Columbia. The fiddleheads and mature fronds are moderately important food sources for several species of wildlife, including deer, bear, elk, moose, and caribou.

Blechnum spicant (L.) Sm.
Polypodiaceae (Polypody Family)

Indicator Value/Significance to Forest Management

Deer fern is a shade-tolerant/intolerant, oxylophytic fern that is a good indicator of acidic, nitrogen poor soils supporting mor humus development and having fresh to very moist soil moisture regimes. The occurrence of this species decreases with increasing continentality, due mainly to its acute sensitivity to frost. It prefers hypermaritime to submaritime, subalpine-boreal, and summer-wet, cool-mesothermal climates. Deer fern is scattered to abundant (occasionally dominant) in the Coast Forest Region, where it occurs in old-growth coniferous forests on water-receiving sites and, less frequently and vigorously, on water-collecting sites. Although it is a conspicuous species in the understory of densely shaded forests, it rarely produces fertile fronds under such conditions. Associated species with similar indicator value include salal, oval-leaved huckleberry (*Vaccinium ovalifolium* Sm.), and lanky moss. It often occurs in the same habitats as sword fern, but prefers slightly wetter, more acidic soils.

	Poor	Medium	Rich
Wet			
Moist	▓		
Fresh	▓		
Dry			

Distribution and Habitat

Distribution: British Columbia, along the coast and in the coastal mountain ranges. Also inland in the Revelstoke region.

Habitat: On well-decomposed organic materials in swamps, moist woods, cliffs, and springy banks; prefers calcium poor soils.

Deer Fern
Blechnum commun

Description

General: Perennial fern growing to about 1 m tall; fronds arising from a short, creeping, woody rhizome; several sterile fronds form a circular crown around fewer fertile fronds.

Fronds: Sterile fronds **(a)** once-divided (pinnate), evergreen, leatherlike, with pinnae 2–5 mm wide; fertile fronds **(b)** deciduous, longer than the sterile fronds, and with narrower pinnae.

Reproductive Structures: Spores produced in linear sori along the margins of the pinnae of the fertile fronds, covering the entire lower surfaces of the pinnae.

Phenology: Fertile fronds develop in summer.

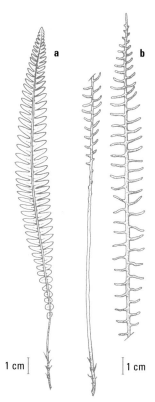

1 cm

1 cm

Cystopteris bulbifera (L.) Bernh.
Polypodiaceae (Polypody Family)

Indicator Value/Significance to Forest Management

Bulblet fern is a shade-tolerant/intolerant fern that is a good indicator of rich, calcareous soils with mull or moder humus forms and fresh to moist soil moisture regimes. It occurs on water-receiving sites, where it is common in moist, shady woods and in seepage zones associated with calcareous cliffs. When growing in large colonies, especially under conifers, bulblet fern benefits the site by increasing nutrient cycling and adding nutrient rich organic matter to the soil.

	Poor	Medium	Rich
Wet			
Moist			■
Fresh			■
Dry			

Distribution and Habitat

Distribution: Northwestern Ontario, east to Nova Scotia and the west coast of Newfoundland. Bulblet fern has been designated as a rare species in Newfoundland.

Habitat: Wet, shaded rocks, ledges, talus slopes, ravines, and moist woodlands; mainly on calcareous soils.

Bulblet Fern
Cystoptéride bulbifère

Description

General: A tufted fern with graceful, arching fronds, mostly 30–80 cm tall, arising from a short, stout rhizome; usually growing in large colonies, often forming a significant part of the ground cover.

Fronds: Fertile fronds, delicate, lanceolate with a long-attenuated tip, not narrowed at the base, stalk much shorter than the blade; sterile fronds smaller; veins on the pinnules mostly ending in a notch or sinus at the margin; in early spring, the bright maroon-colored stalks are conspicuous.

Reproductive Structures: Spores produced in sori on the undersides of the pinnules **(a)**; sori few, scattered, away from the margins of the pinnules; indusia brownish, hoodlike, rounded or truncate at the apex; dark green bulblets often borne near the apex of the blade on the undersides of the pinnae; bulblets drop off and develop into new plants.

Phenology: Spores mature in early summer.

a
1 cm

1 cm

Dryopteris spinulosa (O.F. Muell.) Watt
Polypodiaceae (Polypody Family)

Indicator Value/Significance to Forest Management

Spinulose wood fern is a good indicator of nutrient medium, fresh to very moist, mineral soils. Soils associated with this species are often characterized by friable mor and acidic moder humus forms. Spinulose wood fern is primarily an acidophilic species of shaded forest habitats where it occupies water-shedding and water-receiving sites under boreal, cool-temperate, and cool-mesothermal climatic regimes. Its frequency of occurrence increases with increasing precipitation. In the Boreal Forest Region, spinulose wood fern shows high regional presence values for white spruce–balsam fir stands located east of the Manitoba border. In the Lesser Slave Lake area in north-central Alberta, this species is characteristic of poorly drained, alluvial or lacustrine sites. In southern boreal wetland habitats in Ontario, it is associated with seepage areas in cedar swamps having well-decomposed peaty soils. In the Great Lakes–St. Lawrence Forest Region of Ontario, this species occurs most abundantly in relatively open, hardwood–hemlock forest ecosystems on moderately fertile, wet, organic soils. Farther east, in the northern hardwood forests of Quebec, spinulose wood fern is characteristic of mesic sites associated with glaciated knobs and moderately deep till slopes supporting sugar maple and yellow birch stands; however, it is not considered to be a good site indicator in this region. Associated species with similar indicator values include naked mitrewort and one-flowered pyrola.

Large colonies of spinulose wood fern can adversely affect young conifer crops by shading out seedlings, by competing for rooting space, and by causing smothering and snow-press damage to germinants and newly planted seedlings. The species maintains site productivity through active recycling of nutrient rich litter.

	Poor	Medium	Rich
Wet			
Moist		▓	
Fresh		▓	
Dry			

Distribution and Habitat

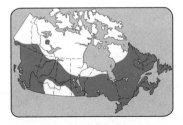

Distribution: Southern Yukon, British Columbia, east through central Saskatchewan, central and southern Manitoba, Ontario, to Labrador, Nova Scotia, and Newfoundland.

Habitat: Fresh to moist mineral soils in forest habitats, seepage zones, swamps, and rocky slopes.

Spinulose Wood Fern
Dryoptéride spinuleuse

Description

General: Medium to large, lacy, usually evergreen, woodland fern. Fronds growing in a circular cluster from a stout, creeping or erect rhizome; leaf stalks are continuous with the rhizome, not jointed.

Fronds: Erect, mostly spreading from the center of the cluster, 30–80 cm or more tall; blade lanceolate to narrowly triangular, divided 2 or 3 times (bi- to tripinnate); stalk shorter than the blade and covered with ovate, brown scales; pinnules lanceolate to oblong with spine-tipped teeth.

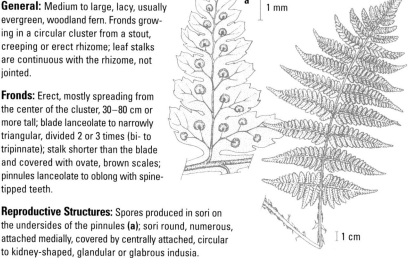

a   1 mm

1 cm

Reproductive Structures: Spores produced in sori on the undersides of the pinnules (a); sori round, numerous, attached medially, covered by centrally attached, circular to kidney-shaped, glandular or glabrous indusia.

Phenology: Spores mature in mid- to late summer.

Synonyms: This very variable species complex has recently undergone a name change to *Dryopteris carthusiana* (Vill.) H.P. Fuchs, an earlier validly published name, and has also been subdivided into several new species. For more information see Cody and Britton (1989). In this report, all taxa are included together under the widely used name *D. spinulosa*. Also known as *D. austriaca* (Jacq.) Woynar ex Schinz & Thell. var. *spinulosa* (Muell.) Fiori.

Notes   The rhizomes of spinulose wood fern have traditionally been collected, steamed, and eaten in the fall by aboriginal peoples in British Columbia. The fronds are commonly used by florists as greenery to accent bouquets.

Equisetum sylvaticum L.
Equisetaceae (Horsetail Family)

Indicator Value/Significance to Forest Management

Woodland horsetail, a shade-tolerant, oxylophytic species, is an indicator of moist to wet soils. It occurs across a wide range of soil nutrient conditions. Most commonly, wood-land horsetail is associated with mildly acidic, nitrogen poor soils on water-receiving sites, where the soils tend not to be saturated (some seep-age may be present). These are usually gleysolic or organic soils with mor humus forms, typically supporting coniferous forest vegetation. This species

	Poor	Medium	Rich
Wet	▓	▓	▓
Moist	▓	▓	▓
Fresh			
Dry			

is less common on water-collecting sites, such as floodplains and forested fens. On these sites woodland horsetail is associated with nutrient rich, often calcareous soils, generally under wet conditions. It is often found in association with an extensive moss mat and woodland sedge species. Woodland horsetail is widely distributed under continental, boreal, and cool-temperate climatic conditions, and increases in frequency with increasing continentality. It shows high presence values for black spruce stands throughout the Boreal Forest Region, except in the Yukon and in Atlantic Canada. Less frequently, it occurs in white spruce—balsam fir stands. In boreal wetland habitats in Ontario, this species is associated with hardwood swamps on alluvial sites having neutral to slightly basic, nutrient rich, silt and clay-textured soils, and is a sensitive indicator of minerotrophy. In the Great Lakes—St. Lawrence Forest Region of Quebec, woodland horsetail occurs in white elm—black ash stands on wet, bottomland alluvial flats and lower slopes, usually below 210 m elevation, and in areas underlain by limestone.

Distribution and Habitat

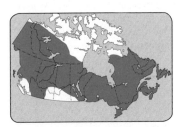

Distribution: Yukon and northern British Columbia, east to Labrador and Newfoundland.

Habitat: Moist to wet, open woods, wet banks, swamps and meadows; on both mineral and organic soils.

Woodland Horsetail
Prêle des bois

Description

General: Erect, delicate, lacy, woodland horsetail, with separate sterile and fertile stems; arising from deep, shiny, light brown, creeping rhizomes.

Stems: Annual; jointed at the nodes (a) as are all horsetails; sterile and fertile stems distinct: sterile stems (b) green, slender (1.5–3 mm thick), to 70 cm tall, hollow; sheaths at the nodes inflated, green at the base, with chestnut brown tips, united into 3–4 groups of triangular teeth; upper two-thirds of the stem with whorled branches from well-spaced nodes, branches spreading, drooping, and bearing secondary branches; fertile stems (c) shorter, thicker, with larger sheaths, initially unbranched and brownish in color, becoming green and producing a few, small branches in the upper nodes after the spores are released.

Reproductive Structures: Spores produced in "cones" at the tips of the fertile stems; cones 3 cm long, on long stalks 2–6 cm long, withering after the spores are shed.

Phenology: Spores mature and are released in April or May.

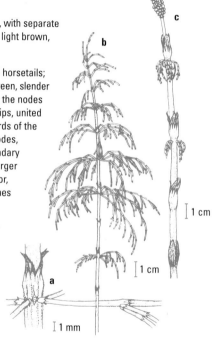

Notes

Although woodland horsetail is an interesting and attractive plant, it is not easily cultivated because of difficulty in transplanting. Natural dyes can be made from woodland horsetail. Horsetails, in general, are known as scouring rushes because their silica-containing stems were once useful for cleaning dishes and pots. Early reports that horsetails were bioaccumulators of gold have not been substantiated; however, there is ample evidence that these plants do bioaccumulate zinc.

Gymnocarpium dryopteris (L.) Newm.
Polypodiaceae (Polypody Family)

Indicator Value/Significance to Forest Management

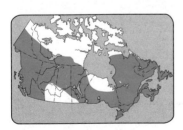

Oak fern is a shade-tolerant, nitrophytic indicator species of nutrient rich, fresh to very moist soils that support the development of moder and mull humus forms. It is scattered to plentiful in forest habitats on water-receiving sites (floodplain, seepage, and stream-bank) under boreal, cool-temperate, and cool-mesothermal climatic regimes. In British Columbia, its frequency of occurrence increases with increasing precipitation and continentality, and decreases with increasing temperature. In the Boreal Forest Region east of Manitoba, oak fern is most prevalent

	Poor	Medium	Rich
Wet			
Moist			▓
Fresh			
Dry			

in white spruce–balsam fir stands. In the southern Boreal Forest Region in Ontario, this species is also associated with tall-shrub thicket swamps in riparian habitats having well-decomposed organic soils with some accumulation of silt. Farther south, in the upland hardwood forests of the Great Lakes–St. Lawrence Forest Region, oak fern shows greater ecological amplitude, occurring on drier, infertile to very fertile soils on protected, cool, humid sites, becoming very abundant where the stands are semi-open; here, it is less common on wet soils and in wetlands. In the western section of this forest region, oak fern indicates rich, moist, circumneutral, fine-textured soils. Species with similar indicator values include lady fern, devil's club, rose twisted stalk (*Streptopus roseus* Michx.), and one-leaved foamflower (*Tiarella unifoliata* Hook.).

Distribution and Habitat

Distribution: Yukon and British Columbia, east to Labrador and Newfoundland. Subspecies *disjunctum* (Rupr.) Sarvela is restricted to British Columbia and is generally larger (up to 50 cm tall) than the more widespread subspecies *dryopteris*.

Habitat: Cool rocky woods, swamp margins, shaded slopes, especially in the Boreal Forest Region.

Oak Fern
Gymnocarpe fougère-du-chêne

Description

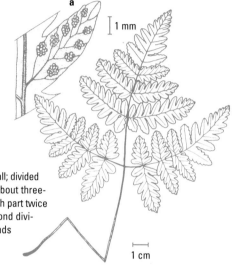

a

1 mm

1 cm

General: Small, delicate, woodland fern with distinctive 3-parted triangular blades held horizontal to the ground; arising singly from a slender, forking, black, long-creeping rhizome; new fronds produced throughout the growing season, the first fronds unfolding early in spring at about the same time as leaf flush occurs in deciduous trees of the overstory; often forming patches in moist depressions in open woods.

Fronds: Thin, broadly triangular, up to 30 cm tall; divided into 3 parts, the lower 2 parts opposite and about three-quarters as long as the central upper part; each part twice divided (bipinnate); pinnae on the 2 lateral frond divisions unequal, lower of each pair larger; fronds glandless or nearly so; bright lime to yellow-green; stalk slender, straw-colored, dark at the base, longer than the blade, with a few scales.

Reproductive Structures: Spores produced in sori on the undersides of the pinnules (**a**); sori small, round, lacking indusia, situated near the margins of the pinnules.

Phenology: Spores mature in mid- to late summer.

Synonym: *Dryopteris disjuncta* (Rupr.) Morton

Lycopodium lucidulum Michx.
Lycopodiaceae (Clubmoss Family)

Indicator Value/Significance to Forest Management

Shining clubmoss is a shade-tolerant species characteristic of fresh to moist, nitrogen rich soils with neutral to basic soil reaction. It occurs on water-receiving sites where it is common in cool, shaded woods. In the Boreal Forest Region, this species occurs sporadically in white spruce–balsam fir stands near Lake Superior and in Atlantic Canada, but is absent or infrequent in black spruce stands. In the southern part of the Boreal Forest Region in Ontario, shining clubmoss is associated with tall-shrub thicket swamps in riparian habitats having

	Poor	Medium	Rich
Wet			
Moist			▓
Fresh			▓
Dry			

well-decomposed organic soils with some accumulation of silt. In upland hardwood–hemlock forest ecosystems in the Great Lakes–St. Lawrence Forest Region, shining clubmoss is indicative of moist to wet soils over a range of soil fertility, from infertile to somewhat fertile. It is also abundant in hemlock-dominated stands on protected, humid sites with poorly drained soils. Farther east, in the northern hardwood forests of Quebec, shining clubmoss is indicative of mesic sites associated with glaciated knobs and moderately deep till slopes supporting sugar maple and yellow birch stands. This species is often associated with rose twisted stalk (*Streptopus roseus* Michx.), spinulose wood fern, and beaked hazel. Species with similar indicator values include white baneberry (*Actaea pachypoda* Ell.), red baneberry, beaked hazel, and bristly black currant.

Distribution and Habitat

Distribution: Southern Manitoba, northwestern Ontario to southern Ontario, east along the St. Lawrence River valley to eastern New Brunswick, Prince Edward Island, Nova Scotia, and Newfoundland. Shining clubmoss has been designated as a rare species in Manitoba; in the United States, it is rare in Arkansas, Illinois, Iowa, and Missouri.

Habitat: Cool, moist, rich coniferous and hardwood forests, on streambanks, and on swamp margins.

Shining Clubmoss
Lycopode brillant

Description

General: Perennial, evergreen clubmoss, with spreading, horizontal stems running along the surface of the ground and ascending, simple to few-forked, branches, up to 25 cm tall; each year's new growth indicated by a narrow zone of shorter leaves along the stem or branch.

Leaves: Tightly spiralling around the stems and branches; appearing whorled and 6-ranked **(a)**; oblanceolate, widest above the middle, 7–15 mm long, bristle-tipped **(b)**; dark, glossy green; spreading to deflexed; margins slightly toothed to smooth.

Reproductive Structures: Yellow, kidney-shaped, sporangia borne in the axils of short, lower leaves **(c)**; reproductive buds (gemmae) often borne in the axils of longer upper leaves **(d)**.

Phenology: Spores mature in late summer.

Synonym: *Huperzia lucidula* (Michx.) Rothm.

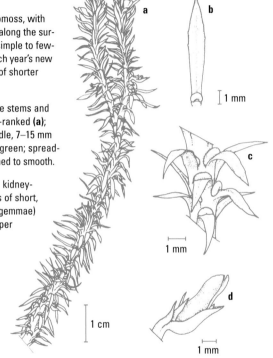

Notes

Spores of various *Lycopodium* species have been used to make fireworks; each spore contains a small fat reserve which burns with a brief but violent flash. The spores were also formerly used like talc to lubricate rubber goods.

Onoclea sensibilis L.
Polypodiaceae (Polypody Family)

Indicator Value/Significance to Forest Management

Sensitive fern is a shade-tolerant/intolerant fern that is a good indicator of periodically flooded, nutrient rich sites with moist to wet, mainly clay-textured soils. It is found primarily on water-receiving sites in low-lying areas, in full sun or shade, in thickets or at the edges of woods, usually adjacent to water. In the southern Boreal Forest Region in Ontario, this species is associated with tall-shrub thicket swamps in riparian habitats having well-decomposed organic soils with some accumulation of silt. In the northern hardwood forests of Quebec, this

species is characteristic of white elm−sugar maple and white elm−black ash stands on moist to wet, bottomland alluvial soils. Sensitive fern is often associated with such species as blue cohosh (*Caulophyllum thalictroides* [L.] Michx.), spotted touch-me-not (*Impatiens capensis* Meerb.), and wood nettle.

Distribution and Habitat

Distribution: Southern Manitoba, east through Ontario and Quebec to the Maritimes and Newfoundland.

Habitat: Rich, moist to wet habitats in woodlands, meadows, wetlands, and along lakeshores.

Sensitive Fern
Onoclée sensible

Description

General: Medium-sized, somewhat coarse fern with distinctly different sterile and fertile fronds borne on slender, creeping rhizomes; forming loose clumps, the smaller, darker, fertile fronds surrounded by larger, leafy, sterile fronds.

Fronds: Sterile fronds **(a)** up to 80 cm tall, with broad, triangular blades that tilt upwards and backwards, blades 12–30 cm long, 15–30 cm wide, once-divided (pinnate), lower pinnae with wavy margins, the central axis becoming broadly winged towards the tip; fertile fronds **(b)** shorter than the sterile fronds, with pinnae much contracted, greenish but becoming blackish at maturity, modified and inrolled to form bead-like reproductive structures.

Reproductive Structures: Spores produced in sori that are wrapped into bead-like clusters on the pinnae of the fertile fronds.

Phenology: Spores mature in late summer and early fall.

1 cm

b   a

Notes   Sickness and death of horses have been reported after ingestion of hay containing sensitive fern.

Osmunda claytoniana L.
Osmundaceae (Royal Fern Family)

Indicator Value/Significance to Forest Management

Interrupted fern is a shade-tolerant/intolerant fern characteristic of moist, subacid to neutral soils with moderately low levels of nitrogen. It is found on the lower end of water-receiving sites in semi-open, deciduous and mixed forests, often along zones of seepage and on streambanks. It is sometimes associated with cinnamon fern (*O. cinnamomea* L.), a closely related species with similar indicator value. In upland hardwood–hemlock ecosystems within the Great Lakes–St. Lawrence Forest Region, inter-rupted fern is indicative of moist to wet, poorly drained, mineral soils with a wide range of soil fertility conditions. In these habitats it is often associated with bearded shorthusk grass (*Brachyelytrum erectum* [Schreb.] Beauv.).

	Poor	Medium	Rich
Wet			
Moist		■	
Fresh			
Dry			

Distribution and Habitat

Distribution: Southeastern Manitoba, east through Ontario and Quebec, to the Maritimes and New-foundland, with isolated populations in Labrador and northern Quebec.

Habitat: Moist habitats on wooded slopes, wetland margins, riverbanks, and open thickets.

Interrupted Fern
Osmonde de Clayton

Description

General: Large, coarse fern with fronds up to 120 cm tall, arching outwards from a central cluster; the middle, spore-bearing pinnae of fertile fronds much smaller than the sterile pinnae, giving an interrupted appearance to the frond.

Fronds: Blades almost twice-divided (sub-bipinnate); pinnules **(a)** with rounded to acute tips, each lower edge overlapping the upper edge of the next lower pinnule; sterile fronds arching outwards, shorter than the more erect fertile fronds; fertile fronds **(b)** with 2–4 middle pairs of smaller, dark green, fertile pinnae, turning dark brown at maturity.

Reproductive Structures: Spores produced in clusters on specialized, contracted pinnae in the middle of fertile fronds.

Phenology: Spores mature in late summer.

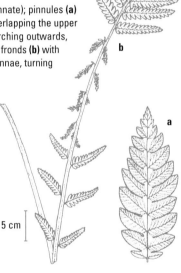

b

a

5 cm

1 cm

Notes   Interrupted fern is an attractive, easily cultivated fern that is not weedy or invasive and is suitable for the garden.

Polystichum munitum (Kaulf.) K. Presl
Polypodiaceae (Polypody Family)

Indicator Value/Significance to Forest Management

Sword fern is a shade-tolerant/intolerant, nitrophytic fern characteristic of nutrient rich, moist but strongly drained, seepage soils with moder and mull humus forms. This species indicates base-rich parent materials. It is frequent to abundant (often dominant) on water-receiving sites, particularly on those enriched by the surface flow of fine organic materials, and sporadic to scattered on water-shedding sites. Sword fern is widespread in forest understories and, being tolerant of light, may persist when a stand is harvested. Its frequency of occurrence

	Poor	Medium	Rich
Wet			
Moist			▓
Fresh			
Dry			

decreases with increasing elevation and continentality. Species with a similar indicator value include vanilla leaf, dull Oregon-grape, and three-leaved foamflower. On Vancouver Island, a ground cover of sword fern and vanilla leaf indicates high site quality for the growth of Douglas-fir (*Pseudotsuga menziesii* [Mirb.] Franco).

Although sword fern is a dominant understory species on some of British Columbia's most productive sites for Douglas-fir and other conifers, it is not considered to be a serious competitor. However, it does interfere with conifer regeneration and growth in localized areas. Its presence on a site may result in competition for moisture and light, and provide habitat for tree-damaging mammals. However, the magnitude of these effects has not been studied.

Distribution and Habitat

Distribution: Coastal and southern British Columbia, with isolated populations in the central and northern regions of the province.

Habitat: Moist, humus rich, coniferous forests and shaded slopes.

Sword Fern
Polystic à épées

Description

General: Coarse, usually large fern, with once-divided (pinnate), evergreen fronds, 20–150 cm tall; fronds arising from a stiffly erect crown at the head of a stout, woody, scaly rhizome; often forming extensive colonies.

Fronds: Blade linear-lanceolate, once-divided (pinnate); pinnae linear and long-pointed, margins smooth to sharply fine-toothed, each pinna with a prominent tooth or lobe on its upper side adjacent to the stalk; stalk densely scaly.

Fruiting Structures: Spores produced in sori on the undersides of the pinnae **(a)**; sori large, situated midway between the pinna margin and midvein, covered by round, fringe-margined indusia.

Phenology: Spores mature in August.

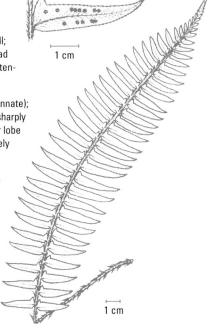

a

1 cm

1 cm

Notes   Sword fern is eaten by wildlife when population densities are high and preferred food sources are limited. The large rhizomes have been used as emergency food by British Columbia aboriginal peoples. Portions of the plant have also been used medicinally as a cure for diarrhea.

Mosses
and
Lichens

Aulacomnium palustre (Hedw.) Schwaegr.
Aulacomniaceae (Bog Moss Family)

Indicator Value/Significance to Forest Management

Ribbed bog moss is a shade-intolerant species that is an excellent indicator of nutrient medium, moist to wet soils. It is characteristic of wetland, mineral gleysolic, and organic soils in non-forested, semi-terrestrial communities on water-receiving sites. This species is also found in open-canopy forests on water-collecting sites where the groundwater table during the growing season is at or above the ground surface, except during the driest months of the summer. It has strong affinity for humus and mineral soil but avoids wood and bark. In the Aspen–Oak

and Manitoba Lowlands Sections of the Boreal Forest Region in southern Manitoba, where the underlying soils are calcareous, ribbed bog moss is characteristic of poorly drained sites dominated by black spruce and tamarack. In wetland habitats in the southern part of the Boreal Forest Region in Ontario, this species is associated with seepage areas in cedar swamps having well-decomposed peaty soils. In the western Great Lakes–St. Lawrence Forest Region, ribbed bog moss occupies the driest parts of bog hummocks, often replacing brown bog sphagnum when the bog is undergoing a drying trend.

Distribution and Habitat

Distribution: Nearly cosmopolitan, occurring across Canada.

Habitat: Very common and widespread in wetland habitats such as fens, bogs, marshes, wooded swamps, and wet meadows, often in thickets on pond margins and along streams; tolerant of a wide range of soil pH levels.

Ribbed Bog Moss
Aulacomnie des marais

Description

General: Erect, fairly robust moss, not glossy; in loose or dense, yellow-green tufts, 5–10 cm deep; branches rare; stems green, matted with red rhizoids among the leaves, sterile stems often bearing clusters of triangular-shaped buds at the ends of the stem or branches.

Leaves: Erect-spreading on the stem; 2–4 mm long, keeled, lanceolate **(a)**, twisted and contorted when dry; midrib distinct as a pale green ridge, ending below the leaf tip.

Reproductive Structures: Sporophytes borne singly at the apex of the main stems; setae 25–45 mm long, strongly twisted when dry; capsule red-brown, strongly inclined to horizontal, curved, deeply fur-rowed when dry, 2.5–4 mm long.

Phenology: Spores mature from late autumn to early spring.

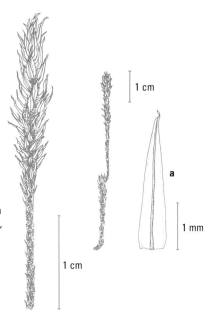

1 cm

1 cm

a

1 mm

Cladina spp.
Cladoniaceae (Cladonia Family)

Indicator Value/Significance to Forest Management

Reindeer lichens are good indicators of acidic, nutrient poor, extremely dry to very dry soils. These soils tend to be coarse-textured and shallow, and are typically associated with mor humus forms. In wet areas and peatlands, reindeer lichens occupy (micro-) topographic prominences subject to regular desiccation, such as the tops of sphagnum hummocks. Reindeer lichens are commonly found in open-canopy forests in northern Canada on strongly drained, water-shedding sites under tundra, boreal, cool-temperate, and cool-mesothermal climatic

regimes. In west-central Alberta, an abundant cover of reindeer lichens is indicative of poor site conditions for lodgepole pine (*Pinus contorta* Dougl. ex Loud. var. *latifolia* Engelm.). In the boreal wetlands of northern Ontario, reindeer lichens are associated with the tops of sphagnum hummocks in oligotrophic, shrub rich, treed bogs. In upland, hardwood–hemlock forest ecosystems in the Great Lakes–St. Lawrence Forest Region, gray reindeer lichen is indicative of exposed sites with thick, acid humus forms and very dry to dry, infertile soils.

Distribution and Habitat

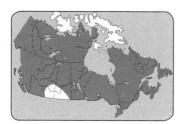

Distribution: Transcontinental, except for the southern prairies.

Habitat: Occurring on dry, acidic, mineral and humus substrates, less often on decaying wood; in tundra, open woods, heath barrens, rock outcrops, and peatlands. *Cladina stellaris* tends to prefer the driest sites, especially those with infertile sand or bedrock substrates, compared with *C. mitis*, *C. arbuscula*, and *C. rangiferina,* which occupy a broader range of soil and site conditions.

Reindeer Lichens • Caribou Lichens
Lichens à caribous

Description

General: Erect, "shrubby" (fruticose) ground lichen, to about 10 cm tall; consisting of white to pale yellow or grayish green branching structures (podetia) **(a)**. Branches few to numerous, hollow and round in cross-section, and very brittle when dry; often covering the ground with extensive colonies of intertwined branches. *Cladina* species lack the small scale-like "squamules" found in most *Cladonia* lichens.

a

1 mm

Cladina stellaris (Opiz) Brodo (northern reindeer lichen): White to pale yellowish-gray, very finely branched; consisting of discrete, compact, cauliflower-like heads, which may be separate or aggregated into loose colonies that cover the ground.

1 cm

C. arbuscula

Cladina arbuscula (Wallr.) Hale & W. Culb. (yellow reindeer lichen): Yellowish or greenish-gray, with distinct main branches and fewer side branches compared with *C. stellaris*; forming scattered entangled masses on the ground but not discrete heads; axils of the branches are open and the branch tips are strongly pointed in one direction as if windswept.

1 cm

C. stellaris

Cladina mitis (Sandst.) Hale & W. Culb. (green reindeer lichen, not illust.): Similar to *C. arbuscula* but branch tips not strongly oriented in one direction.

Cladina rangiferina (L.) Harm. (gray reindeer lichen, not illust.): Ashy-gray; forming scattered, tangled masses of branches but not distinct cauliflower-like heads.

Notes   Reindeer lichens are important as forage for many northern animals including reindeer, caribou, muskox, and moose. The forage value varies with the season and place, with utilization being greatest in midwinter when other food sources are scarce.

Climacium dendroides (Hedw.) Web. & Mohr
Climaciaceae (Tree Moss Family)

Indicator Value/Significance to Forest Management

Tree moss is a shade-tolerant moss characteristic of nitrogen rich, moist to wet, organic soils. It occurs at the edge of fens, in forested areas (particularly cedar-dominated forests), and in calcareous tundra habitats. Tree moss is apparently indifferent to soil pH levels. Species with similar indicator values include ribbed bog moss, electrified cat's tail moss (*Rhytidiadelphus triquetrus* (Hedw.) Warnst.), and several species of *Mnium* moss. In the Aspen—Oak and Manitoba Lowlands Sections of the Boreal Forest Region in southern Manitoba, where the underlying

	Poor	Medium	Rich
Wet			▓▓
Moist			▓▓
Fresh			
Dry			

soils are calcareous, tree moss is characteristic of poorly drained sites dominated by black spruce and tamarack. In the northern hardwood forests of Quebec, this species occurs on wet, bottomland alluvial flats and lower slopes, usually below 210 m elevation, and in areas underlain by limestone and supporting American elm—black ash stands.

Distribution and Habitat

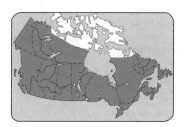

Distribution: Circumboreal, Yukon and British Columbia, east to Quebec, Labrador and Newfoundland.

Habitat: Shady, swampy woods, along streams and lakeshores; mainly on organic soils and decaying logs.

Tree Moss
Climacie arbustive

Description

General: Erect, tree-like moss arising from creeping stems that are partially or wholly underground, new shoots produced each year; branches spreading, flexuous; plants dark green to yellowish-green, shiny when dry, forming loose mats 3–9 cm tall.

Leaves: Stem leaves heart-shaped, 4–4.5 mm long, 2–2.5 mm wide, clasping and overlapping on the reddish-brown stem; branch leaves **(a)** smaller, 2–3 mm long, 1 mm wide; midrib apparent on all leaves as a reddish ridge on the back of the leaf.

Reproductive Structures: Uncommon; sporophytes borne on short shoots among the branches, often several on one plant; setae red, smooth, twisted when dry, 1.8–4.5 mm long; capsules erect, cylindrical, about 3–4 mm long.

Phenology: Spores mature during the summer.

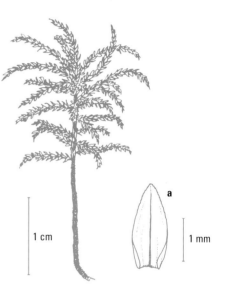

1 cm

a

1 mm

Hylocomium splendens (Hedw.) BSG
Hylocomiaceae (Hylocomium Family)

Indicator Value/Significance to Forest Management

Although stair-step moss is a humus-loving species, having a strong affinity for needles and detritus on the forest floor and found only rarely on mineral soil, it is a good indicator of sites with acidic, nutrient poor, fresh to wet soils. It is abundant and often dominant on the forest floors of coniferous forests on water-receiving sites. It is found on sites that are character-ized by mor humus forms, developed under boreal, temperate, and mesothermal climatic regimes. On the prairies, it is commonly found in association with tree moss, ribbed bog moss, and several spe-

	Poor	Medium	Rich
Wet	▓		
Moist	▓		
Fresh	▓		
Dry			

cies of the moss genus *Mnium* on fen and muck soils in conifer forests. On nutrient rich sites, stair-step moss grows on decaying coniferous wood. In British Columbia, its frequency of occur-rence decreases with increasing elevation and temperature. Associated west coast species with similar indicator values include deer fern, false azalea, white-flowered rhododendron, and red huckleberry. In wetland habitats in the southern part of the Boreal Forest Region in Ontario, this species is associated with seepage areas in cedar swamps having well-decomposed, peaty soils. In general, stair-step moss is a ubiquitous species in white spruce−balsam fir and black spruce stands throughout the Boreal Forest Region, and is typically one of the dominant ground-covering feathermosses. On moist soils with moderate drainage, development of the feathermoss stratum comes with stand age and is rarely complete until the stands are more than 70 years old.

Feathermosses stabilize the forest floor by preventing or minimizing soil erosion on steep slopes and by helping to maintain soil moisture levels. They also absorb nitrogen and other ele-ments from rainfall, and on decomposing are an important source of mineral nutrition for trees. Feathermoss carpets provide poor seedbed environments in cutovers because they dry out rapidly, resulting in low seed germination and seedling survival of crop trees. Such sites often require scarification to the mineral soil.

Distribution and Habitat

Distribution: Widespread across Canada.

Habitat: On humus, mineral soils, and rocks, less often on rotting wood, in fresh or wet coniferous forests.

Stair-Step Moss
Hylocomie brillante

Description

General: Relatively robust, olive-green to yellowish or brownish, mat-forming feathermoss of delicate appearance; having regular, bi-tripinnate, planar branching and a step-like appearance due to each year's new shoot developing from the middle of the upper surface of the previous season's growth; stems and branches stiff and wiry, red, covered with tiny green scales; often forming extensive mats with other forest floor feathermoss species.

a   b

1 mm

Leaves: Stem leaves (**a**) loosely erect and overlapping, 2–3 mm long, concave, broadly oblong-ovate, with 2 short midribs, abruptly narrowed to a short or long, often wrinkled, point; branch leaves (**b**) smaller, oblong-lanceolate, sharp-tipped.

1 cm

Reproductive Structures: Uncommon; sporophytes scattered along the stems; setae reddish, smooth; capsules brown, ovate to cylindrical, inclined, somewhat constricted below the mouth when dry.

Phenology: Spores mature in the spring.

Notes   This species is easily recognized by the step-like layers formed as a result of the annual growth pattern of the fronds; poor specimens may be confused with **Schreber's moss** (*Pleurozium schreberi* [Brid.] Mitt.), but the latter species lacks small green scales on its main branches.

When growing in extensive mats over the forest floor of rich, moist woods stair-step moss, with its regular, planar branching and stair-step growth habit, is one of Canada's most beautiful mosses.

Kindbergia oregana (Sull.) Ochyra
Brachytheciaceae (Ragged Moss Family)

Indicator Value/Significance to Forest Management

Oregon beaked moss is a shade-tolerant indicator of nutrient poor to nutrient medium, moderately dry to fresh soils in the Coast Forest Region. It is a common and often dominant forest floor moss in the early successional stages of Douglas-fir, grand fir, western white pine, and western redcedar forests on water-shedding sites. Its frequency of occurrence decreases with increasing elevation, precipitation, and continentality. Commonly associated species include vanilla

	Poor	Medium	Rich
Wet			
Moist			
Fresh	▓	▓	
Dry	▓		

leaf, salal, stair-step moss, dull Oregon-grape, and lanky moss. The interwoven mats of this species help to protect the forest soils from raindrop erosion, particularly on steep slopes.

Distribution and Habitat

Distribution: Endemic to western North America; in Canada found only in British Columbia, where it is common in coastal areas but uncommon in the interior.

Habitat: Sea level to subalpine coniferous forests.

Oregon Beaked Moss
Kindbergie de l'Oregon

Description

General: Pinnately branching, creeping, woodland moss, forming interwoven mats; youngest shoots slightly arching upwards from older reclining shoots; stems 5–30 cm long.

Leaves: Stem leaves **(a)** heart-shaped, with a long narrow point, broad basal portion slightly clasping the stem; standing perpendicular to the stem with the tip pointing upwards; midrib single, about two-thirds the length of the leaf. Branch leaves **(b)** similar but smaller, with acute tips.

Reproductive Structures: Sporophytes scattered along the stems; setae rough to touch, red-brown; capsule ovate **(c)**, nodding to inclined, often somewhat constricted below the mouth when dry.

Phenology: Sporophytes appear in late autumn; the spores mature in the spring.

Synonyms: *Stokesiella oregana* (Sull.) Robins., *Eurhynchium oreganum* (Sull.) Jaeg. & Sauerb

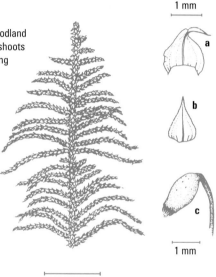

1 mm

a

b

c

1 mm

1 cm

Ptilium crista-castrensis (Hedw.) De Not.
Hypnaceae (Hypnum Family)

Indicator Value/Significance to Forest Management

Plume moss, although a humus-loving feathermoss with a strong affinity for needles and detritus on the forest floor and only rarely found on mineral soil, is a shade-tolerant, oxylophytic species with good indicator value for sites having acidic, nutrient poor, dry to moist soils with mor humus forms. It tends to occur in areas of the forest where snows persist longest. Plume moss occurs on water-shedding and water-receiving sites and is found in virtually all forest habitats. It reaches its best development in closed-canopy, coniferous forests where it often

forms extensive ground mats in association with other feathermosses. Plume moss is a ubiquitous species in white spruce–balsam fir and black spruce stands throughout the Boreal Forest Region and is typically one of the dominant ground-covering feathermosses. In wet habitats in the Northern Clay Section of the Boreal Forest Region in northern Ontario, this species is a sensitive indicator of minerotrophy. Species with similar indicator values, and which often co-occur with plume moss, include bluebead lily (*Clintonia borealis* [Ait.] Raf.), queen's cup (*C. uniflora* [Schult.] Kunth), bunchberry (*Cornus canadensis* L.), mountain box (*Pachistima myrsinites* [Pursh] Raf.), mountain huckleberry (*Vaccinium membranaceum* Dougl.), stair-step moss, Schreber's moss (*Pleurozium schreberi* [Brid.] Mitt.), lanky moss, and electrified cat's tail moss (*Rhytidiadelphus triquetrus* [Hedw.] Warnst.).

Feathermoss carpets provide poor seedbed environments in cutovers because they dry out rapidly. This results in low seed germination and seedling survival of crop tree species. On these sites, it is often necessary to scarify the forest floor down to mineral soil in preparation for regeneration.

Distribution and Habitat

Distribution: Circumpolar in the northern hemisphere, occurring across Canada.

Habitat: Rotting wood, humus, and mineral soil in virtually all forest types.

Plume Moss • Knight's Plume Moss
Hypne cimier

Description

General: Robust, rigid, plume-like, yellow-green feathermoss; growing in tight, extensive mats on the forest floor or intermixed with other feather-mosses such as Schreber's moss (*Pleurozium schreberi* [Brid.] Mitt.) and stair-step moss; easily recognizable by the strikingly regular and plumose branching, with the branches approximately equal in length except at the triangular-shaped tip of the plant.

Leaves: Stem leaves (**a**) larger than the branch leaves, 2–3 mm long, ovate-triangular, with a long, narrow, curled tip; branch leaves (**b**) up to 2 mm long, narrower than the stem leaves, with long, pointed tips that are curved strongly downwards.

Reproductive Structures: Sporophytes scattered individually along the stems; setae reddish and smooth, twisted when dry; capsules reddish-brown, cylindrical, tapering into the setae, horizontally inclined, strongly curved when mature.

Phenology: Spores mature from late summer to fall.

Synonym: *Hypnum crista-castrensis* Hedw.

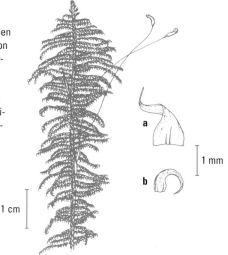

1 cm

1 mm

a

b

Notes The specific epithet refers to a soldier's plume; this moss is also known as knight's plume moss.

Rhytidiadelphus loreus (Hedw.) Warnst.
Hylocomiaceae (Hylocomium Family)

Indicator Value/Significance to Forest Management

Lanky moss is a shade-tolerant, humicolous, oxylophytic moss having different ecological indicator values in western and eastern Canada (see distribution map). In western Canada, lanky moss is characteristic of nutrient poor, fresh to moist soils and is a good indicator of strong acidity in the humus. It occurs in hyper-maritime to submaritime, subalpine-boreal, and cool-mesothermal climatic regimes, with its frequency of occurrence increasing with increasing elevation and continentality. In eastern Canada, its presence indicates nutrient medium to nutrient rich,

	Poor	Medium	Rich
Wet			
Moist			
Fresh			
Dry			

fresh to moist soils in submaritime, boreal, and cool-mesothermal climatic regimes. In both regions, it occurs on water-shedding and water-receiving sites, where it is plentiful to abundant in closed-canopy, coniferous forests. In the boreal forest, it shows a high regional presence value for white spruce–black spruce stands in Newfoundland; elsewhere, it is rare or absent in this forest type. Associated species in western Canada include deer fern, spinulose wood fern, Alaskan blueberry (*Vaccinium alaskaense* Howell), red huckleberry, and the moss *Plagiothecium undulatum* (Hedw.) BSG. In eastern Canada, common associates include spinulose wood fern, oval-leaved huckleberry (*V. ovalifolium* Sm.), stair-step moss, plume moss, Schreber's moss (*Pleurozium schreberi* [Brid.] Mitt.), and electrified cat's tail moss (*Rhytidiadelphus triquetrus* [Hedw.] Warnst.).

Distribution and Habitat

Distribution: Interrupted circumboreal distribution; in western Canada—British Columbia, reported from the Yukon and Alberta; in eastern Canada—Nova Scotia, Labrador and Newfoundland, reported from Ontario and Quebec.

Habitat: Logs, humus and mineral soils in coniferous forests.

Lanky Moss
Rhytidiadelphe lanière

Description

General: Relatively robust moss, forming dense, interwoven, glossy, bright green to yellowish-green mats up to 15 cm thick; stems orange-red, irregularly to regularly pinnately branched, stem tips curved.

Leaves: Stem leaves **(a)** 3.5–4 mm long, broadly ovate at the base, abruptly narrowing to a long, slender, channelled tip bending back sharply at the middle of the leaf; branch leaves **(b)** similar to the stem leaves in shape but smaller.

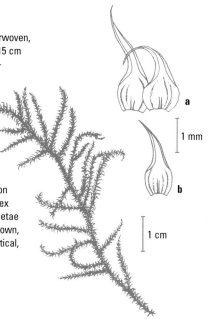

a

1 mm

b

1 cm

Reproductive Structures: Sporophytes occurring on lateral shoots, shoots arising well back from the apex of the main stems, several sporophytes per shoot; setae reddish-brown, twisted when dry; capsules reddish-brown, ovoid to nearly spherical, somewhat inclined from vertical, 2–3 mm long, tapering to the setae.

Phenology: Spores mature in the spring.

Sphagnum fuscum (Schimp.) Klinggr.
Sphagnaceae (Peat Moss Family)

Indicator Value/Significance to Forest Management

Brown bog sphagnum is a shade-intolerant, oxylophytic, peat-forming moss of open, semi-terrestrial habitats with nitrogen poor, acidic, organic soils and high water tables. Within these habitats, however, it has a local affinity for dry microsites and is characteristically found growing on the tops of hummocks.

This species is often associated with goldthread, Labrador-tea, northern starflower (*Trientalis arctica* Fisch. ex Hook.), and small cranberry. Other species of the genus *Sphagnum* with similar indicator values include *S. nemoreum* Scop., *S. fallax* (Klinggr.)

	Poor	Medium	Rich
Wet	■		
Moist			
Fresh			
Dry			

Klinggr., *S. papillosum* Lindb., and *S. tenellum* (Brid.) Pers. ex Brid. Brown bog sphagnum is the dominant sphagnum moss in the forested wetlands of Alberta. In the Hudson Bay Lowlands of northern Ontario, this species becomes established when soil conditions change from minerotrophic to ombrotrophic.

Black spruce—sphagnum swamps that are dominated by brown bog sphagnum are poor sites for tree growth. Although the slow-growing, compact mounds of this species provide good seedbeds for seed germination and seedling survival, seedling growth is typically unsuccessful because of the nutrient poor conditions.

Distribution and Habitat

Distribution: Common and widespread, occurring across Canada.

Habitat: Forming dense hummocks or capping older, drier hummocks in hummock-hollow complexes in bogs and black spruce muskeg.

Brown Bog Sphagnum
Sphaigne brune

Description

General: Slender delicate moss **(a)**; heads small, compact; stems brown (not red as in similar species); forming compact, brown or brownish-green tufts or mounds; branches **(b)** slender and thread-like, in clusters of 3–5, with 2 normally spreading and interwoven inside the hummocks; characteristically found on the tops of hummocks.

Leaves: Stem leaves **(c)** tongue-shaped, with fringed, rounded tips, not strongly overlapping; branch leaves **(d)** lanceolate, margins inrolled towards the tip, strongly overlapping.

Reproductive Structures: Uncommon; sporophytes borne singly on the head; capsules small, globular, dark brown or black, on short, erect pseudopodia.

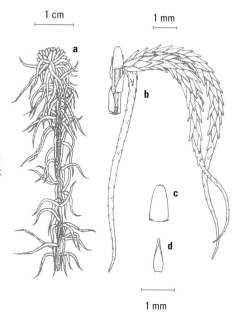

1 cm

1 mm

1 mm

Notes Sphagnum mosses are well known for their high cation-exchange capacity, making them very useful for pollution monitoring. They can be sensitive indicators of airborne pollutants such as sulphur dioxide and gaseous fluorides, and metallic pollutants such as mercury, lead, and copper. Numerous uses are made of dried sphagnum mosses due to their softness and high water absorbency properties. They make excellent emergency dressings for wounds, not only because they are absorbent but also because they are mildly antiseptic. Horticultural uses include the protection of plant roots during transportation, a medium for plant propagation, and a soil conditioner for increasing water retention capability. Sphagnum mosses have been used as packing materials for the shipping of delicate goods. In some regions, dried sphagnum (peat) is a valuable source of domestic fuel.

Sphagnum girgensohnii Russ.
Sphagnaceae (Peat Moss Family)

Indicator Value/Significance to Forest Management

Common green sphagnum is a shade-tolerant moss of wet, acidic, nitrogen poor to medium, mineral gleysolic and organic soils. Like other sphagnum mosses, it is indicative of extremely poor soil drainage and aeration. This species is apparently restricted to shaded coniferous forest habitats on water-receiving sites; it is rarely found in bog and fen habitats. In the southern sections of the Boreal Forest Region and in the Great Lakes–St. Lawrence Forest Region, it is typically found in wet depressions and seepage areas in cedar swamps and in periodically wet,

distinctly calcium rich habitats. In montane regions, it occurs in more acidic situations on rocks, in seepages, and on humic banks. In wet habitats in the Clay Belt Section of the Boreal Forest Region in northern Ontario, common green sphagnum is a sensitive indicator of minerotrophy. In British Columbia, it is often associated with western skunk cabbage, deer fern, and goldthread.

The loose growth form of common green sphagnum constitutes poor seedbed conditions for black spruce (*Picea mariana* [Mill.] BSP). Its rapid rate of growth may outpace tree seedling growth, thus inhibiting successful black spruce regeneration.

Distribution and Habitat

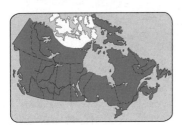

Distribution: Widespread, occurring across Canada but absent on the western and northern arctic islands and adjacent mainland.

Habitat: In shaded, moist to wet forest habitats.

Common Green Sphagnum • Girgensohn's Peat Moss
Sphaigne de Girgensohn

Description

General: Fairly robust moss **(a)**, forming loose, green (never red) mats; branches **(b)** in clusters of 4–5, with 2 of the branches spreading and drooping, clusters arranged in 5 rows along the stem giving the heads a distinctly star-shaped appearance when viewed from above; with a large, glossy, terminal bud protruding from the center of the head.

Leaves: Stem leaves **(c)** broadly tongue-shaped, with a blunt, ragged tip; branch leaves **(d)** ovate, with a pointed tip, upper margins inrolled.

Reproductive Structures: Uncommon; sporophytes borne singly on the head; capsules small, globular, dark brown or black, on short, erect pseudopodia.

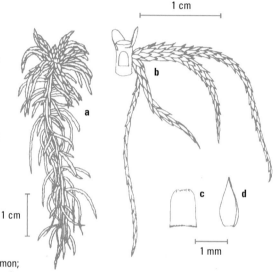

1 cm

1 cm

1 mm

Notes   See general notes on the sphagnum mosses under *Sphagnum fuscum*.

Sphagnum squarrosum Crome
Sphagnaceae (Peat Moss Family)

Indicator Value/Significance to Forest Management

Prickly sphagnum is a shade-tolerant moss of coniferous forests that occurs on rich to very rich sites with wet mineral or shallow organic soils subject to relatively high eutrophic influences through seasonal flooding or fluctuation in the water table. In the mountains of northern British Columbia, this species is found on wet, acidic to circumneutral, rocky slopes, or on cliff ledges in spruce–fir forests. In Alberta, it is rarely found in calcareous regions, occurring in wet, shaded habitats at fen margins, in minerotrophic seepages, and in depressions in spruce

	Poor	Medium	Rich
Wet			▓
Moist			
Fresh			
Dry			

forests. In the Great Lakes–St. Lawrence Forest Region, it is a calciphyte and is especially common in swamps or among larch, alder, and willow thickets along stream margins. Prickly sphagnum is typically associated with pale fat-leaved sphagnum (*S. centrale* C. Jens. ex H. Arnell & C. Jens), common green sphagnum, and brittle-stemmed sphagnum

Distribution and Habitat

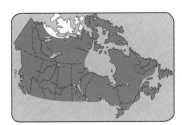

Distribution: Widespread, occurring across Canada but absent in the western and northern arctic islands and adjacent mainland.

Habitat: Wet or seepage areas in shady coniferous forests and swamps.

Prickly Sphagnum
Sphaigne squarreuse

Description

General: Robust, bright green moss **(a)**, 5–10 cm tall, forming loose mats; lateral branches **(b)** in clusters of 5, 2–3 branches wide-spreading, the others pendant along the stem.

Leaves: Stem leaves **(c)** oblong to tongue-shaped, with a broad, rounded, fringed tip; branch leaves **(d)** broadly ovate, concave, narrowing to a pointed tip, the tip bent sharply backwards at the middle of the leaf; the spreading tips of the branch leaves give a characteristic ragged appearance to the plant.

Reproductive Structures: Uncommon; sporophytes borne singly on the head; capsules small, globular, dark brown or black, on short, erect pseudopodia.

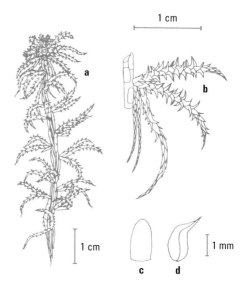

1 cm

1 cm

1 mm

Notes See general notes on the sphagnum mosses under *Sphagnum fuscum*.

Sphagnum wulfianum Girg.
Sphagnaceae (Peat Moss Family)

Indicator Value/Significance to Forest Management

Brittle-stemmed sphagnum is a shade-tolerant, minerotrophic moss that prefers mainly moist to wet, nutrient medium substrates. It is usually found in white cedar and black spruce swamps, rarely occurring with full light exposure. Brittle-stemmed sphagnum can be found occasionally in fresh to moist black spruce stands, where it occupies small hummocks corresponding to stumps or logs in advanced stages of decay. Among sphagnum mosses, this species is one of the most xerophytic. In Alberta, brittle-stemmed sphagnum is indicative of minero-

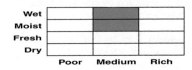

trophic habitats in coniferous forests. Commonly associated species of the *Sphagnum* genus include prickly sphagnum, pale fat-leaved sphagnum (*S. centrale* C. Jens. ex H. Arnell & C. Jens.), common green sphagnum, and *S. russowii* Warnst.

Distribution and Habitat

Distribution: British Columbia and the Northwest Territories (Great Slave Lake area), east to southern Labrador and Newfoundland; reported from Vancouver Island, British Columbia.

Habitat: Coniferous fens and swamps, occasionally in alder and willow thickets, rarely on the margins of open fens.

Brittle-Stemmed Sphagnum
Sphaigne de Wulf

Description

General: Robust, brownish-green moss **(a)**, with large, rounded heads that resemble flowering heads of clover; forming loose tufts; branches **(b)** crowded in clusters of 6–13, with 3 or more spreading, the others pendant along the stem; stem blackish when scraped, wiry, brittle, breaking with an audible snap.

Leaves: Stem leaves **(c)** small, oblong-triangular, tips blunt-pointed, margins smooth or slightly fringed; branch leaves **(d)** lanceolate, tapering to a long tip, widely recurved when dry giving the plant a fuzzy appearance.

Reproductive Structures: Uncommon; sporophytes borne singly on the head; capsules small, globular, dark brown or black, on short, erect pseudopodia.

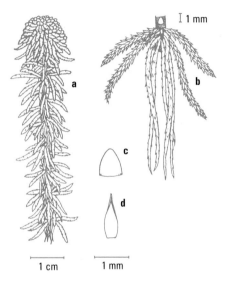

I 1 mm

a

b

c

d

1 cm   1 mm

Notes   See general notes on the sphagnum mosses under *Sphagnum fuscum*.

Thuidium abietinum (Hedw.) BSG
Thuidiaceae (Fern Moss Family)

Indicator Value/Significance to Forest Management

Wiry fern moss is a shade-intolerant moss having good indicator value for dry, calcareous substrates. It occurs on water-shedding sites, where it is found on exposed rocks, mineral soil, the sandy surfaces of partially stabilized dunes,

	Poor	Medium	Rich
Wet			
Moist			
Fresh			
Dry			

and among talus at the base of cliffs, and on water-receiving sites, where it is found on humus in open, coniferous forests. Other species with similar indicator values include soapberry, and the mosses *Hypnum revolutum* (Mitt.) Lindb. and *Tortula ruralis* (Hedw.) Gaertn., Meyer & Sherb.

Distribution and Habitat

Distribution: Widespread across Canada, except on Prince Edward Island.

Habitat: Dry, exposed rocks, mineral soil, talus, on humus in open, coniferous stands.

Wiry Fern Moss
Thuidie petit-sapin

Description

General: Robust, rigid feathermoss with wiry stems up to 12 cm high; usually forming dense, dark green, yellowish, or dark brown tufts; stems and branches loosely pinnate.

Leaves: Stem leaves **(a)** broadly ovate, with a long, tapering tip, erect when dry, erect-spreading when moist, midrib extending three-quarters or more of the leaf length; branch leaves **(b)** similar but smaller, with an acute tip, not long-tapering.

Reproductive Structures: Uncommon; sporophytes scattered along the stems, well back from the stem apex; capsules narrowly cylindrical, curved, inclined from the vertical.

Synonym: *Abietinella abietina* (Hedw.) Fleisch.

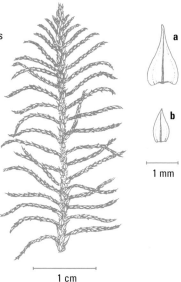

a

b

1 mm

1 cm

Glossary of Selected Terms

-A-

achene: a dry simple one-seeded fruit

acidophilic (plant): adapted to and thriving in acidic soils

allelopathic (plant): the biological influence of a plant on nearby plants; often an inhibition of germination or growth

alluvial (soil): composed of sand, silt, or clay materials deposited by running water

anthesis: the period from the opening of a flower to fruit set

aril: a fleshy attachment entirely or partially covering an associated seed

awn: a stiff, bristle-like appendage at the tip of the glume and lemma of many grasses

- B -

biennial: a plant requiring 2 years to complete its life cycle; often growing vegetatively the first year, fruiting and dying the second

bipinnate: twice pinnate; leaflets borne on axes that branch from a central axis

blade: the flattened, expanded portion of a leaf or frond

bog: an acidic, permanently flooded heath and sphagnum-covered wetland

boreal (climate): a cold, snowy climate with severe winters and short cool summers; having 1 to 3 months with an average temperature above 10°C and the coldest month with an average temperature below −3°C.

bract: a modified leaf attached below the stalk of a solitary flower or an inflorescence

bracteole: a modified leaf attached below the stalk of a single flower in an inflorescence

bulb: a modified thickened underground stem consisting of fleshy scale-like leaves

bulblet: an outgrowth that detaches from a fern frond and develops into a new plant

- C -

calcareous: containing calcium carbonate; rich in lime

calciphyte: a plant adapted to and thriving in calcium-rich soils

calyx: the outermost whorl of a flower, consisting of the sepals

catkin: a flexible elongated inflorescence that bears unisexual flowers

chlorotic: pale and yellowish, symptomatic of reduced chlorophyll development

circumneutral (soil): almost neutral, having a pH between 6.5 and 7.5

colluvial (soil): derived from rock, sand, and soil and deposited at the base of a slope

continental (climates): climates of the interior mainland east of the British Columbia coastal mountain ranges; typified by cold winters and warm to hot summers

continentality: the degree of influence exerted by interior continental air masses on climate, increasing as oceanic influences decrease

cool-mesothermal (climate): a mesothermal climate with cool summers and the warmest month with an average temperature below 22°C

cool-temperate (climate): a temperate climate with cool summers and the warmest month with an average temperature below 22°C

corolla: the inner set of floral leaves, the petals

crenate: with shallow, rounded, irregular teeth

cuneate: wedge-shaped, tapering to a narrow base

–D–

decumbent: reclining on the ground with the tip upturned

deflexed: bent downward

drupe: a fleshy, indehiscent fruit with the seed enclosed in a hard ovary wall

–E–

ecotone: a transitional zone between two diverse vegetation communities

edaphic: resulting from or influenced by soil rather than by climate

eutrophic: rich in minerals, bases, and essential plant nutrients

exfoliating: peeling or scaling off in thin layers

–F–

fen: wetland typified by mineral-rich alkaline waters, supporting mostly non-sphagnum mosses

fern: flowerless, seedless plant bearing divided leaf-like fronds and reproducing by spores

field (water) capacity: the water content of a soil after being saturated by rainfall or irrigation and allowed to drain

flexuous: having turns or windings; curving alternately in opposite directions

follicle: a dry fruit consisting of a single carpel

friable: easily crumbling and breaking into small pieces

fruticose: shrubby, erect and branching; a growth form of lichens

–G–

glabrous: without hairs

glaucous: covered or whitened with a bloom

gleyed (soil): mottled in appearance indicating periodic saturation and reduction

gleysolic (soil): associated with a high groundwater table or temporary saturation above a relatively impermeable soil layer

glume: a chaff-like bract at the base of a grass spikelet

graminoid: a member of the grass family Gramineae or, in general use, any narrow-leafed grass-like plant

grasses: members of the family Gramineae; mostly herbaceous plants with jointed stems, slender leaves, and flowers borne in spikelets

–H–

heath, heathland: open terrain dominated by ericaceous shrubs

herb: a seed-producing plant lacking woody tissue and annually dying back to ground level

humus: the organic portion of soil, formed from decomposed and amorphous plant or animal matter

hypermaritime (climates): climates of the outer coastal areas of British Columbia under the dominant influence of the Pacific Ocean; typified by modest extremes of temperature in both summer and winter

-I-

indusium (indusia): a membranous epidermal growth covering the sorus

inflorescence: a cluster of small flowers on a common stalk

involute: rolled inward or toward the upper side

-K-

keeled: having a raised central ridge

-L-

lacustrine (sites): areas with soils composed of stratified sediments of water-borne sand, silt, or clay, formed by settlement from suspension or by wave action

lanceolate: longer than wide, broadest below the middle, tapered towards the tip

lemma: lower of a pair of bracts enclosing a single flower in the inflorescence of a grass

lenticel: a raised corky structure in the bark of woody plants that facilitates gas exchange

lichen: a composite plant consisting of a fungus living in symbiosis with an alga

ligule: an outgrowth from the upper and inner side of a grass leaf blade where it joins the stem

linear: much longer than wide, sides parallel

-M-

maritime (climates): climates of British Columbia coastal areas west of the coastal mountains, under the prevailing influence of the Pacific Ocean

marsh: a wetland, periodically inundated by slow-moving or standing water; characterized by emergent reeds, sedges, and grasses

mesothermal (climate): mild, rainy climate with moderate seasonal variation; having 8 or more months with an average temperature above 10°C and the coldest month with an average temperature below 18°C but above −3°C.

minerotrophic: dependent on water-borne nutrients for enrichment

moder: humus layer 5 cm or less deep, consisting of partly decomposed organic matter with some organic structures discernible; partly mixed with mineral soil by soil fauna activity

montane (habitat): hills or mountain slopes between lowlands and elevations having a subalpine-boreal climate

mor: humus layer 5 cm or more deep, compacted by fungal mycelia, consisting of partly decomposed organic matter with some organic structures (leaves, twigs) discernible

moss: nonvascular rootless plants (Bryophyta) with small leafy, often tufted stems

mull: humus layer 5 cm or less deep, consisting of well-humidified organic matter; well-mixed with the mineral soil by soil fauna activity

mycorrhiza: symbiotic association between the mycelium of a fungus and the roots of a plant

-N-

node: point of origin of a leaf or bud on a stem

nitrophyte: a plant requiring a soil rich in nitrogen—**nitrophytic**

–O–

oblanceolate: longer than broad, broadest above the middle, tapered towards the tip

oblong: longer than broad, rectangular, sides parallel

obovate: inversely ovate, broadest above the middle

oligotrophic: deficient in minerals, bases, and essential plant nutrients

ombrotrophic: dependent on rain-borne nutrients for enrichment

ovate: egg-shaped, broadest below the middle

oxylophyte: a plant that prefers or is restricted to acid soils—**oxlyophytic**

–P–

panicle: an inflorescence consisting of a central axis with branches bearing stalked flowers

peat: fully and partially decomposed plant material accumulated under wet, anaerobic conditions

pinna (pinnae): a first-order leaflet or division on a frond or compound leaf

pinnate (leaf/frond): leaflets arranged in 2 rows along a central axis; feather-like

pinnule: second-order leaflet or division on a frond or compound leaf

podetium (podetia): simple or branched upright hollow structure on certain lichens

podzolized: referring to soils in which mineral and organic substances have been leached from surface layers and precipitated or flocculated farther down in the soil profile

pseudopodium (pseudopodia): in sphagnum mosses, a leafless branch resembling the seta and bearing the capsule

–R–

raceme: an inflorescence consisting of a central axis bearing stalked flowers

receptacle: the enlarged end of a flower stalk on which some or all of the flower parts are borne

recurved: curving downward or backward

reflexed: abruptly turning downward

rhizoid: a simple cellular filament, analogous to a root

rhizome: an elongated horizontal underground stem

riparian: describing the immediate environment of a natural watercourse

–S–

samara: indehiscent winged fruit

scurfy: having a roughened, particulate surface

sedge: marsh plants of the family Cyperaceae, especially those in the genus *Carex*

seral: series of stages in an ecological succession

sessile: stalkless

seta (setae): in bryophytes, a short stalk connecting the sporophyte foot and capsule

shrub: a spreading, multistemmed woody perennial, generally less than 4.5 m high

sinus: the gap between two adjacent lobes of a leaf

sorus (sori): a cluster of sporangia located on the fertile fronds of ferns

spadix: a fleshy, club-shaped axis bearing flowers, generally enveloped by a spathe

spathe: a leaf-like bract enclosing an inflorescence

spike: an inflorescence consisting of a central axis bearing sessile flowers

spikelet: a grouping of grass flowers arranged in a spike or in a panicle that bears spikes as branches

sporangium (sporangia): a structure in which spores are formed

sporophyte: an individual of the diploid generation; in bryophytes, the minor part of the life cycle

squamule: a small scale-like structure making up the body of certain lichens

stamen: the pollen-bearing organ of a flowering plant

stigma: the part of a flower pistil that receives pollen

stoloniferous: having basal branches that, on contact with soil, produce roots and shoots

style: the part of a flower pistil that connects the stigma and ovary

subalpine (habitat): mountainous terrain at high elevations below the tree line

subalpine-boreal (climate): cold, snowy; distinguished from a typical boreal climate by temperature and precipitation characteristics of high, mountainous areas

sub-bipinnate: somewhat or nearly bipinnate

submaritime (climates): climates of the British Columbia coastal interior just inland from the coastal mountains and under the strong influence of the Pacific Ocean

submontane (habitat): mountain bases, lowland plains, or bottomlands

subtend: to attach immediately beneath

suture: a seam along which a fruiting structure splits and opens

swamp: a wooded wetland seasonally covered by slow-moving or standing water

sward: an extensively grass-covered area of land

-T-

talus: loose fragmented rock material accumulated at the foot of a cliff or steep slope

temperate (climate): a cold, snowy climate with well-defined seasons varying greatly in precipitation and temperature; having 4 to 7 months with an average temperature above 10°C and the coldest month with an average temperature below −3°C.

tillers: shoots developing from adventitious or axillary buds at the base of a stem

tree: an upright, single-stemmed woody perennial, generally more than 4.5 m in height

tripinnate: term for a bipinnate frond on which the pinnules are further subdivided

truncate: abruptly ending, appearing cut off

tundra (climate): a polar climate; having all months with an average temperature below 10°C, 9 to 11 months with an average temperature below 0°C, and at least 1 month with an average temperature above 0°C permitting sparse, low vegetation.

-U-

umbel: an umbrella-shaped inflorescence consisting of many stalked flowers all attached at the distal point of a common stalk

–V–

valve: the unit into which a pod or capsule divides

–W–

wet-temperate (climate): temperate climate with no distinct dry season

whorled: having 3 or more leaves arising at a single stem node

–X–

xerophytic: plant adapted for growth in environments with a limited water supply

References

Addison, P.A.; Puckett, K.J. 1980. Deposition of atmospheric pollutants as measured by lichen element content in the Athabasca Oil Sands area. *Canadian Journal of Botany* 58:2323–2324.

Armson, K.A. 1977. *Forest Soils: Properties and Processes*. University of Toronto Press, Toronto. 390 p.

Bailey, L.H.; Bailey, E.Z. Compilers. 1976. *Hortus Third: A Concise Dictionary of Plants Cultivated in the United States and Canada*. Macmillan Publishing Company, New York. 1290 p.*

Baldwin, K.A.; Sims, R.A. 1989. *Field Guide to the Common Forest Plants in Northwestern Ontario*. Forestry Canada/Ontario Ministry of Natural Resources. 344 p.*

Bell, F.W. 1991. *Critical Silvics of Conifer Crop Species and Selected Competitive Vegetation in Northwestern Ontario*. COFRDA Report 3310/NWOFTDU Technical Report 19. Ontario Ministry of Natural Resources Publication 4531. 177 p.*

Boufford, D.E. 1982. The systematics and evolution of *Circaea* (Onagraceae). *Annals of the Missouri Botanical Garden* 69(4):804–994.*

Buse, L.J.; Bell, F.W. 1992. *Critical Silvics of Selected Crop and Competitor Species in Northwestern Ontario*. Ontario Ministry of Natural Resources. 138 p.*

Cajander, A.K. 1926. The theory of forest types. *Acta Forestalia Fennica* 29:1–108.

Calder, J.A.; Taylor, R.L. 1968. *Flora of the Queen Charlotte Islands*. Part 1: *Systematics of the Vascular Plants*. Monograph 4. Canada Department of Agriculture, Ottawa. 659 p.*

Canadian Soil Survey Committee, Subcommittee on Soil Classification. 1978. *The Canadian System of Soil Classification*. Publication 1646. Canada Department of Agriculture, Ottawa. 164 p.

Carlisle, D.; Berry, W.L.; Kaplan, I.R.; Watterson, J.R. Editors. 1986. *Mineral Exploration: Biological Systems and Organic Matter*. Vol. 5. Prentice-Hall, Englewood Cliffs, N.J.

Carmean, W.H. 1975. Forest site quality evaluation in the United States. *Advances in Agronomy* 27:209–269.

Cobb, B. 1963. *A Field Guide to the Ferns and Their Related Families*. The Peterson Field Guide Series. Houghton Mifflin Co., Boston. 281 p.*

Cody, W.J.; Britton, D.M. 1989. *Ferns and Fern Allies of Canada*. Publication 1829/E. Agriculture Canada, Ottawa. 430 p.*

Coile, T.S. 1938. Forest classification: classification of forest sites with special reference to ground vegetation. *Journal of Forestry* 36:1062–1066.

Comeau, P.G.; Comeau, M.A.; Utzig, G.F. 1982. *A Guide to Plant Indicators of Moisture for Southeastern British Columbia, with Engineering Interpretations*. British Columbia Ministry of Forests, Victoria. 119 p.*

Corns, I.G.W.; Annas, R.M. 1986. *Field Guide to Forest Ecosystems of West-Central Alberta*. Canadian Forestry Service, Northern Forestry Centre, Edmonton. 251 p.

Corns, I.G.W.; Pluth, D.J. 1984. Vegetational indicators as independent variables in forest growth prediction in west-central Alberta, Canada. *Forest Ecology and Management* 9:13–25.*

Crum, H.A.; Anderson, L.E. 1981. *Mosses of Eastern North America*. Vols. 1–2. Columbia University Press, New York. 1328 p.*

Daubenmire, R. 1976. The use of vegetation in assessing the productivity of forest lands. *Botanical Review* 42:115–143.

Dore, W.G.; McNeill, J. 1980. *Grasses of Ontario*. Monograph 26. Agriculture Canada, Ottawa. 566 p.*

Farrar, J.L. 1995. *Trees in Canada*. Canadian Forest Service, Natural Resources Canada, Ottawa/Fitzhenry & Whiteside, Markham, Ont. 502 p. + x*

Fernald, M.L. 1950. *Gray's Manual of Botany*. 8th ed. D. Van Nostrand Co., New York. 1632 p.*

Furlow, J.J. 1979. The systematics of the American species of *Alnus* (Betulaceae). Parts 1–2. *Rhodora* 81:1–121, 151–248.*

Fyles, F. 1920. *Principal Poisonous Plants of Canada*. Bulletin 39. Canada Department of Agriculture, Ottawa. 112 p.*

Gleason, H.A. 1952. *The New Britton and Brown Illustrated Flora of the Northeastern United States and Adjacent Canada*. Vols. 1–3. Hafner Press, New York. 1732 p.*

Green, R.N.; Marshall, P.L.; Klinka, K. 1989. Estimating site index of Douglas-fir (*Pseudotsuga menziesii* (Mirb.) Franco) from ecological variables in southwestern British Columbia. *Forest Science* 35:50–63.*

Grout, A.J. 1903. *Mosses with Hand-Lens and Microscope*. 1972 Reprint by Eric Lundberg, Augusta, W.Va. 416 p.*

Haeussler, S.; Coates, D; Mather, J. 1990. *Autecology of Common Plants in British Columbia: A Literature Review*. FRDA Report 158. Forestry Canada/British Columbia Ministry of Forests. 272 p.*

Hale, M.E. 1979. *How to Know the Lichens*. 2nd ed. Wm. C. Brown Co., Dubuque, Iowa. 226 p.*

Harlow, M.H.; Harrar, E.S.; Hardin, J.W.; White, F.M. 1991. *Textbook of Dendrology*. 7th ed. McGraw-Hill, New York. 501 p.

Hawksworth, D.L.; Rose, F. 1970. Qualitative scale for estimating sulphur dioxide air pollution in England and Wales uses epiphytic lichens. *Nature* (London) 227:145–148.

Hazard, H.E. 1937. Plant indicators of pure white pine sites in southern New Hampshire. *Journal of Forestry* 35:477–486.

Heimburger, C.C. 1934. *Forest Type Studies in the Adirondack Region*. Cornell University Agriculture Experimental Station Memoir 156. Cornell University Press, Ithaca, N.Y.

Hitchcock, C.L.; Cronquist, A. 1973. *Flora of the Pacific Northwest*. University of Washington Press, Seattle. 730 p.*

Hosie, R.C. 1979. *Native Trees of Canada*. 8th ed. Canadian Forestry Service, Ottawa/Fitzhenry & Whiteside, Markham, Ont. 380 p.*

Hubbard, W.A. 1969. *The Grasses of British Columbia*. British Columbia Provincial Museum Handbook No. 9. Victoria. 205 p.*

Hultén, E. 1969. *Flora of Alaska and Neighboring Territories*. Stanford University Press, Stanford, Calif. 1008 p.*

Ireland, R.R.; Brassard, G.R.; Schofield, W.B.; Vitt, D.H. 1987. Checklist of the mosses of Canada II. *Lindbergia* 13:1–62*

Johnson, D.; Kershaw, L.; MacKinnon, A.; Pojar, J. 1995. *Plants of the Western Boreal Forest & Aspen Parkland*. Canadian Forest Service, Natural Resources Canada/Lone Pine Publishing, Edmonton. 392 p.*

Jones, R.K.; Pierpoint, G.; Wickware, G.M.; Jeglum, J.K.; Arnup, R.W.; Bowles, J.M. 1983. *Field Guide to Forest Ecosystem Classification for the Clay Belt, Site Region 3E*. Ontario Ministry of Natural Resources. 161 p.

Kimmins, J.P. 1987. *Forest Ecology*. Macmillan, New York. 531 p.

Klinka, K.; Krajina, V.J.; Ceska, A.; Scagel, A.M. 1989. *Indicator Plants of Coastal British Columbia*. University of British Columbia Press, Vancouver. 288 p.*

Krajina, V.; Klinka, K.; Whorrall, J. 1982. *Distribution and Ecological Characteristics of Trees and Shrubs of British Columbia*. University of British Columbia Press, Vancouver, B.C. 130 p.

Lakela, O. 1965. *A Flora of Northeastern Minnesota*. University of Minnesota Press, Minneapolis. 541 p.*

La Roi, G.H.; Strong, W.L.; Pluth, J.D. 1988. Understory plant community classifications as predictors of forest site quality for lodgepole pine and white spruce in west-central Alberta. *Canadian Journal of Forest Research* 18:875–887.*

Looman, J.; Best, K.F. 1979. *Budd's Flora of the Canadian Prairie Provinces*. Publication 1662. Agriculture Canada, Ottawa. 863 p.*

Luttmerding, H.A.; Demarchi, D.A.; Dea, E.C; Meidinger. D.V.; Vold, T. 1990. *Describing Ecosystems in the Field*. Manual II, 2nd ed. British Columbia Ministry of Environment, Victoria. 213 p.

Mallik, A.U. 1987. Allelopathic potential of *Kalmia angustifolia* to black spruce (*Picea mariana*). *Forest Ecology and Management* 20:43–51.

Marie-Victorin, Fr. 1964. Flore Laurentienne. Deuxième édition. Les Presses de l'Université de Montréal, Montréal. 925 p.*

McKay, S.M.; Catling, P.M. 1979. *Trees, Shrubs and Flowers to Know in Ontario*. J.M. Dent and Sons, Toronto. 208 p.*

Meades, W.J.; Moores, L. 1989. *Forest Site Classification Manual: A Field Guide to the Damman Forest Types of Newfoundland*. FRDA Report 003. Forestry Canada/ Newfoundland and Labrador Department of Forestry and Agriculture.

Moss. E.H. 1959. *Flora of Alberta*. University of Toronto Press, Toronto. 546 p.*

Mueller-Dombois D. 1964. The forest habitat types of southeastern Manitoba and their application to forest management. *Canadian Journal of Botany* 42:1417–1444.

Nieboer, E.; Richardson D.H.S.; Tomassini, F.D. 1978. Mineral uptake and release by lichens: an overview. *Bryologist* 81:226–246.

Payandeh, B. 1986. *Predictability of Site Index from Soil Factors and Lesser Vegetation in Northern Ontario Forest Types*. Information Report O-X-373. Great Lakes Forestry Center, Canadian Forestry Service, Sault Ste. Marie, Ont.

Porsild, A.E.; Cody, W.J. 1980. *Vascular Plants of Continental Northwest Territories, Canada*. National Museum of Natural Sciences, Ottawa. 667 p.*

Pregitzer, K.S.; Barnes, B.V. 1982. The use of ground flora to indicate edaphic factors in upland ecosystems of the McCormack Experimental Forest, Upper Michigan. *Canadian Journal of Forest Research* 12:661–672.*

Puckett, K.J.; Finegan, E.J. 1980. An analysis of the element content of lichens from the Northwest Territories, Canada. *Canadian Journal of Botany* 58:2073–2089.

Rehder, A. 1940. *Manual of Cultivated Trees and Shrubs.* Vol. 1. *Biosystematics, Floristic & Phylogeny Series.* 2nd ed. Reprinted 1990 by Dioscorides Press, Portland, Oreg. 996 p.

Robinson, B.; Feller, M.C.; Klinka, K. 1982. Four common mosses as indicators of forest floor acidity in the coastal Western Hemlock Zone of southwestern British Columbia. *Syesis* 15:17–23.*

Roland, A.E.; Smith, E.C. 1969. *The Flora of Nova Scotia.* The Nova Scotia Museum, Halifax. 746 p.*

Rowe, J.S. 1956. Uses of undergrowth plant species in forestry. *Ecology* 37(3):461–473.

Rowe, J.S. 1972. *Forest Regions of Canada.* Publication No. 1300. Department of Fisheries and Environment, Canadian Forestry Service, Ottawa. 172 p.

Rowe, J.S. 1992. The ecosystem approach to forestland management. *The Forestry Chronicle* 68:222–224.

Ryan, A.G. 1978. *Native Trees and Shrubs of Newfoundland and Labrador.* Newfoundland and Labrador Department of Tourism, St. John's, Nfld. 116 p.*

Schofield, W.B. 1969. *Some Common Mosses of British Columbia.* Handbook 28. British

Columbia Provincial Museum, Victoria. 262 p.*

Scoggan, H.J. 1957. *Flora of Manitoba.* Bulletin 140, Biological Series 47. National Museum of Canada, Ottawa. 619 p.*

Scoggan, H.J. 1978. *The Flora of Canada.* Parts 1–4. Publications in Botany 7. National Museum of Natural Sciences, Ottawa. 1711 p.*

Sims, R.A.; Baldwin, K.A. 1996. *Forest Humus Forms in Northwestern Ontario.* NODA/NFP Technical Report TR-28. Natural Resources Canada, Canadian Forest Service, Great Lakes Forestry Centre, Sault Ste. Marie, Ont.

Sims, R.A.; Towill, W.D.; Baldwin, K.A.; Wickware, G.M. 1989. *Field Guide to the Forest Ecosystem Classification for Northwestern Ontario.* Forestry Canada/Ontario Ministry of Natural Resources. 191 p.

Soper, J.H.; Heimburger, M.L. 1982. *Shrubs of Ontario.* Publication in Life Sciences. Royal Ontario Museum, Toronto. 495 p.*

Strahler, A.N. 1965. *Introduction to Physical Geography.* John Wiley & Sons, New York. 455 p.

Strong, W.L.; Pluth, D.J.; La Roi, G.H.; Corns, I.G.W. 1991. Forest understory plants as predictors of lodgepole pine and white spruce site quality in west-central Alberta. *Canadian Journal of Forest Research* 21:1675–1683.*

Swanson, D.K.; Grigal, D.F. 1989. Vegetation indicators of organic soil properties in Minnesota. *Soil Science Society of America Journal* 53:491–495.*

Szczawinski, A.F. 1962. *The Heather Family (Ericaeae) of British Columbia.* Handbook

19. British Columbia Provincial Museum, Victoria. 205 p.*

Thompson, I.D.; Mallik, A.U. 1989. Moose browsing and allelopathic effects of *Kalmia angustifolia* on balsam fir regeneration in central Newfoundland (Canada). *Canadian Journal of Forest Research* 19:524–526.

Thompson, J.W. 1967. *The Lichen Genus* Cladonia *in North America*. University of Toronto Press, Toronto. 172 p.*

Trewartha, G.T. 1968. *An Introduction to Climate*. 4th ed. McGrawHill, New York. 402 p.

Vander Kloet, S.P. 1988. *The Genus* Vaccinium *in North America*. Publication 1828. Agriculture Canada, Ottawa.*

Voss, E.G. 1972. *Michigan Flora*. Part 1: *Gymnosperms and Monocots*. Cranbrook Institute of Science and University of Michigan Herbarium, Bloomfield Hills. 488 p.*

Walshe, S. 1980. *Plants of Quetico and the Ontario Shield*. University of Toronto Press, Toronto. 152 p.*

Wroe, R.A.; Smoliak, S.; Johnson, A.; Turnbull, M.G. 1979. *Range Pastures in Alberta*. Report No. 86. Alberta Agriculture and Alberta Energy and Natural Resources, Edmonton.

*Source documents for species factsheets.

Appendix

Names of Indicator Plants and Associated Species

English Common Name	Scientific Name	French Common Name
Alaskan blueberry	*Vaccinium alaskaense* Howell	airelle de l'Alaska
American yew	*Taxus canadensis* Marsh.	if du Canada
balsam fir	*Abies balsamea* (L.) Mill.	sapin baumier
balsam poplar	*Populus balsamifera* L.	peuplier baumier
basswood	*Tilia americana* L	tilleul d'Amérique
beaked hazel	*Corylus cornuta* Marsh.	noisetier à long bec
bearberry	*Arctostaphylos uva-ursi* (L.) Spreng.	raisin d'ours
bearded shorthusk grass	*Brachyelytrum erectum* (Schreb.) Beauv.	brachyélytrum dressé
bigleaf maple	*Acer macrophyllum* Pursh	érable à grandes feuilles
black ash	*Fraxinus nigra* Marsh.	frêne noir
black cottonwood	*Populus trichocarpa* Torr. & A. Gray	peuplier de l'Ouest
black crowberry	*Empetrum nigrum* L.	camarine noire
black spruce	*Picea mariana* (Mill.) BSP	épinette noire
blue cohosh	*Caulophyllum thalictroides* (L.) Michx.	caulophylle faux-pigamon
bluebead lily	*Clintonia borealis* (Ait.) Raf.	clintonie boréale
bluejoint grass	*Calamagrostis canadensis* (Michx.) Beauv.	calamagrostide du Canada
bog-laurel	*Kalmia polifolia* Wangenh.	kalmia à feuilles d'andromède
bog-rosemary	*Andromeda glaucophylla* Link	andromède glauque
bracted honeysuckle	*Lonicera involucrata* (Richards.) Banks	chèvrefeuille involucré
bristly black currant	*Ribes lacustre* (Pers.) Poir.	gadellier lacustre
brittle-stemmed sphagnum	*Sphagnum wulfianum* Girg.	sphaigne de Wulf
brown bog sphagnum	*Sphagnum fuscum* (Schimp.) Klinggr.	sphaigne brune
bulblet fern	*Cystopteris bulbifera* (L.) Bernh.	cystoptéride bulbifère
bunchberry	*Cornus canadensis* L.	quatre-temps
bush honeysuckle	*Diervilla lonicera* Mill.	dièreville chèvrefeuille
cinnamon fern	*Osmunda cinnamomea* L.	osmonde cannelle

English Common Name	Scientific Name	French Common Name
cloudberry	*Rubus chamaemorus* L.	chicouté
common green sphagnum	*Sphagnum girgensohnii* Russ.	sphaigne de Girgensohn
common juniper	*Juniperus communis* L.	genévrier commun
common red sphagnum	*Sphagnum capillaceum* (Weiss) Schrank	sphaigne grêle
common wood-sorrel	*Oxalis montana* Raf.	oxalide de montagne
couch-grass	*Agropyron repens* (L.) Beauv.	chiendent
cow-parsnip	*Heracleum lanatum* Michx.	berce laineuse
deer fern	*Blechnum spicant* (L.) Sm.	blechnum commun
devil's club	*Oplopanax horridus* (Sm.) Miq.	aralie épineuse
Douglas-fir	*Pseudotsuga menziesii* (Mirb.) Franco	douglas
dull Oregon-grape	*Mahonia nervosa* (Pursh) Nutt.	mahonia à nervures saillantes
dwarf enchanter's-nightshade	*Circaea alpina* L.	circée alpine
dwarf raspberry	*Rubus pubescens* Raf.	ronce pubescente
(eastern) hemlock	*Tsuga canadensis* (L.) Carrière	pruche du Canada
(eastern) white pine	*Pinus strobus* L.	pin blanc
electrified cat's tail moss	*Rhytidiadelphus triquetrus* (Hedw.) Warnst.	une mousse
Engelmann spruce	*Picea engelmannii* Parry ex Engelm.	épinette d'Engelmann
false azalea	*Menziesia ferruginea* Sm.	menziésie ferrugineuse
false spikenard	*Smilacina racemosa* (L.) Desf.	smilacine à grappes
field horsetail	*Equisetum arvense* L.	prêle des champs
fireweed	*Epilobium angustifolium* L.	épilobe à feuilles étroites
five-stamened mitrewort	*Mitella pentandra* Hook.	mitrelle à cinq étamines
goldthread	*Coptis trifolia* (L.) Salisb.	savoyane
grand fir	*Abies grandis* (Dougl. ex D. Don) Lindl.	sapin grandissime
gray reindeer lichen	*Cladina rangiferina* (L.) Harm.	un lichen*
green alder	*Alnus crispa* (Ait.) Pursh	aulne crispé

English Common Name	Scientific Name	French Common Name
green reindeer lichen	*Cladina mitis* (Sandst.) Hale & W. Culb.	un lichen*
hair cap moss	*Polytrichum juniperinum* Hedw.	une mousse
hairy Solomon's-seal	*Polygonatum pubescens* (Willd.) Pursh	sceau-de-Salomon pubescent
hairy wild rye	*Elymus innovatus* Beal	élyme innovant
holly-grape	*Mahonia repens* Lindl.	mahonia rampant
Hooker's fairybells	*Disporum hookeri* (Torr.) Nicholson	dispore de Hooker
interrupted fern	*Osmunda claytoniana* L.	osmonde de Clayton
jack pine	*Pinus banksiana* Lamb.	pin gris
Labrador-tea	*Ledum groenlandicum* Oeder	lédon du Groenland
lady fern	*Athyrium filix-femina* (L.) Roth	athyrium fougère-femelle
lanky moss	*Rhytidiadelphus loreus* (Hedw.) Warnst.	rhytidiadelphe lanière
large-flowered bellwort	*Uvularia grandiflora* Sm.	uvulaire grandiflore
large-leaved aster	*Aster macrophyllus* L.	aster à grandes feuilles
leatherleaf	*Chamaedaphne calyculata* (L.) Moench	cassandre caliculé
leatherwood	*Dirca palustris* L.	dirca des marais
lesser pyrola	*Pyrola minor* L.	pyrole mineure
a liverwort*	*Barbilophozia floerkei* (Web. & Mohr) Loeske	une hépatique*
a liverwort*	*Bazzania trilobata* (L.) S.F. Gray	une hépatique*
a liverwort*	*Pellia neesiana* (Gott.) Limpr.	une hépatique*
lodgepole pine	*Pinus contorta* Dougl. ex Loud. var. *latifolia* Engelm.	pin tordu latifolié
low sweet blueberry	*Vaccinium angustifolium* Ait.	airelle à feuilles étroites
mayflower	*Epigaea repens* L.	épigée rampante
mniums	*Mnium* spp.	mousses*
moccasin flower	*Cypripedium acaule* Ait.	cypripède acaule
a moss*	*Hypnum revolutum* (Mitt.) Lindb.	une mousse*
a moss*	*Kindbergia praelonga* (Hedw.) Ochyra	une mousse*

English Common Name	Scientific Name	French Common Name
a moss*	*Plagiothecium undulatum* (Hedw.) BSG	une mousse*
a moss*	*Rhytidiopsis robusta* (Hedw.) Broth.	une mousse*
a moss*	*Sphagnum fallax* (Klinggr.) Klingrr.	une sphaigne*
a moss*	*Sphagnum nemoreum* Scop.	une sphaigne*
a moss*	*Sphagnum papillosum* Lindb.	une sphaigne*
a moss*	*Sphagnum russowii* Warnst.	une sphaigne*
a moss*	*Sphagnum tenellum* (Brid.) Pers. ex Brid.	une sphaigne*
a moss*	*Tortula ruralis* (Hedw.) Gaertn., Meyer & Sherb.	une mousse*
mountain box	*Pachistima myrsinites* (Pursh) Raf.	pachistima myrte
mountain cranberry	*Vaccinium vitis-idaea* L. var. *minus* Lodd.	airelle vigne-d'Ida
mountain huckleberry	*Vaccinium membranaceum* Dougl.	airelle à feuilles membraneuses
mountain sweet cicely	*Osmorhiza chilensis* Hook. & Arnott	osmorhize du Chili
mountain-holly	*Nemopanthus mucronata* (L.) Trel.	némopanthe mucroné
naked mitrewort	*Mitella nuda* L.	mitrelle nue
nodding trillium	*Trillium cernuum* L.	trille penché
northern Labrador-tea	*Ledum decumbens* (Ait.) Lodd.	lédon décombant
northern reindeer lichen	*Cladina stellaris* (Opiz) Brodo	un lichen*
northern starflower	*Trientalis arctica* Fisch. ex Hook.	trientale arctique
oak fern	*Gymnocarpium dryopteris* (L.) Newm.	gymnocarpe fougère-du-chêne
one-flowered globeflower	*Trollius laxus* Salisb. var. *albiflorus* A.	Graytrolle à fleur blanche
one-flowered pyrola	*Moneses uniflora* (L.) A. Gray	monésès uniflore
one-leaved foamflower	*Tiarella unifoliata* Hook.	tiarelle unifoliée
Oregon beaked moss	*Kindbergia oregana* (Sull.) Ochyra	kindbergie de l'Oregon
oval-leaved huckleberry	*Vaccinium ovalifolium* Sm.	airelle à feuilles ovées
Pacific crabapple	*Malus fusca* (Raf.) Schneider	pommier du Pacifique

English Common Name	Scientific Name	French Common Name
pale fat-leaved sphagnum	*Sphagnum centrale* C. Jens. ex H. Arnell & C. Jens.	une sphaigne*
pin cherry	*Prunus pensylvanica* L.f.	cerisier de Pennsylvanie
pipsissewa	*Chimaphila umbellata* (L.) Bart.	chimaphile à ombelle
plume moss	*Ptilium crista-castrensis* (Hedw.) De Not.	hypne cimier
poverty grass	*Danthonia spicata* (L.) Beauv.	danthonie à épi
prickly sphagnum	*Sphagnum squarrosum* Crome	sphaigne squarreuse
purple reedgrass	*Calamagrostis rubescens* Buckley	calamagrostide rouge
purple trillium	*Trillium erectum* L.	trille dressé
queen's cup	*Clintonia uniflora* (Schult.) Kunth	clintonie uniflore
red alder	*Alnus rubra* Bong.	aulne rouge
red baneberry	*Actaea rubra* (Ait.) Willd.	actée rouge
red huckleberry	*Vaccinium parvifolium* Sm.	airelle à petites feuilles
red-berry elder	*Sambucus callicarpa* Greene	sureau rouge du Pacifique
red-osier dogwood	*Cornus stolonifera* Michx.	hart rouge
red pine	*Pinus resinosa* Ait.	pin rouge
reindeer lichens	*Cladina* spp.	lichens à caribous
rhodora	*Rhododendron canadense* (L.) Torr.	rhododendron du Canada
ribbed bog moss	*Aulacomnium palustre* (Hedw.) Schwaegr.	aulacomnie des marais
Rocky Mountain maple	*Acer glabrum* Torr.	érable nain
rose twisted stalk	*Streptopus roseus* Michx.	streptope rose
rough-fruited fairybells	*Disporum trachycarpum* (Wats.) Benth. & Hook.	dispore à fruits rugueux
round-leaved sundew	*Drosera rotundifolia* L.	droséra à feuilles rondes
salal	*Gaultheria shallon* Pursh	salal
salmonberry	*Rubus spectabilis* Pursh	ronce remarquable
Schreber's moss	*Pleurozium schreberi* (Brid.) Mitt.	une mousse
Selkirk's violet	*Viola selkirkii* Pursh ex J. Goldie	violette de Selkirk
sensitive fern	*Onoclea sensibilis* L.	onoclée sensible

English Common Name	Scientific Name	French Common Name
sheep-laurel	*Kalmia angustifolia* L.	kalmia à feuilles étroites
shining clubmoss	*Lycopodium lucidulum* Michx.	lycopode brillant
Sitka spruce	*Picea sitchensis* (Bong.) Carrière	épinette de Sitka
Sitka valerian	*Valeriana sitchensis* Bong.	valériane de Sitka
slough sedge	*Carex obnupta* Bail.	carex voilé
small cranberry	*Oxycoccus microcarpus* Turcz.	airelle canneberge
soapberry	*Shepherdia canadensis* (L.) Nutt.	shépherdie du Canada
speckled alder	*Alnus rugosa* (Du Roi) Spreng.	aulne rugueux
spinulose wood fern	*Dryopteris spinulosa* (O.F. Muell.) Watt	dryoptéride spinuleuse
spotted touch-me-not	*Impatiens capensis* Meerb.	impatiente du Cap
spring beauty	*Claytonia caroliniana* Michx.	claytonie de Caroline
squashberry	*Viburnum edule* (Michx.) Raf.	viorne comestible
stair-step moss	*Hylocomium splendens* (Hedw.) BSG	hylocomie brillante
star-flowered false Solomon's-seal	*Smilacina stellata* (L.) Desf.	smilacine étoilée
stream violet	*Viola glabella* Nutt.	violette glabre
sugar maple	*Acer saccharum* Marsh.	érable à sucre
sweet-fern	*Comptonia peregrina* (L.) Coult.	comptonie voyageuse
sweet-scented bedstraw	*Galium triflorum* Michx.	gaillet à trois fleurs
sword fern	*Polystichum munitum* (Kaulf.) K. Presl	polystic à épées
tall Oregon-grape	*Mahonia aquifolium* (Pursh) Nutt.	mahonia à feuilles de houx
tamarack	*Larix laricina* (Du Roi) K. Koch	mélèze laricin
thimbleberry	*Rubus parviflorus* Nutt.	ronce parviflore
three-fruited sedge	*Carex trisperma* Dew.	carex trisperme
three-leaved false Solomon's-seal	*Smilacina trifolia* (L.) Desf.	smilacine trifoliée
three-leaved foamflower	*Tiarella trifoliata* L.	tiarelle trifoliée
tree moss	*Climacium dendroides* (Hedw.) Web. & Mohr	climacie arbustive
trembling aspen	*Populus tremuloides* Michx.	peuplier faux-tremble

English Common Name	Scientific Name	French Common Name
trout lily	*Erythronium americanum* Ker	érythrone d'Amérique
twinflower	*Linnaea borealis* L.	linnée boréale
vanilla leaf	*Achlys triphylla* (Sm.) DC.	achlyde à trois folioles
vine maple	*Acer circinatum* Pursh	érable circiné
western hardhack	*Spiraea douglasii* Hook.	spirée de Douglas
western hemlock	*Tsuga heterophylla* (Raf.) Sarg.	pruche de l'Ouest
western redcedar	*Thuja plicata* Donn ex D. Don	thuya géant
western skunk cabbage	*Lysichitum americanum* Hult. & St. John	lysichiton d'Amérique
western white pine	*Pinus monticola* Dougl. ex D. Don	pin argenté
white baneberry	*Actaea pachypoda* Ell.	actée à gros pédicelles
white birch	*Betula papyrifera* Marsh.	Bouleau à papier
white elm	*Ulmus americana* L.	orme d'Amérique
white-flowered rhododendron	*Rhododendron albiflorum* Hook.	rhododendron à fleurs blanches
white spruce	*Picea glauca* (Moench) Voss	épinette blanche
wild ginger	*Asarum canadense* L.	asaret du Canada
wild lily-of-the-valley	*Maianthemum canadense* Desf.	maïanthème du Canada
wild-raisin	*Viburnum cassinoides* L.	viorne cassinoïde
wild red raspberry	*Rubus idaeus* L.	framboisier sauvage
wild sarsaparilla	*Aralia nudicaulis* L.	aralie à tige nue
wintergreen	*Gaultheria procumbens* L.	thé des bois
wiry fern moss	*Thuidium abietinum* (Hedw.) BSG	thuidie petit-sapin
wood nettle	*Laportea canadensis* (L.) Wedd.	laportéa du Canada
woodland horsetail	*Equisetum sylvaticum* L	prêle des bois
yellow birch	*Betula alleghaniensis* Britt.	bouleau jaune
yellow-cedar	*Chamaecyparis nootkatensis* (D. Don) Spach	chamaecyparis jaune
yellow reindeer lichen	*Cladina arbuscula* (Wallr.) Hale & W. Culb.	un lichen*

*Common name not given in the publication or French common name not available.

Index of French Plant Names

Index